The Problem of Freedom and Determinism

THE PROBLEM OF FREEDOM AND DETERMINISM

ჴ

Edward D'Angelo

University of Missouri Studies Volume XLVIII
University of Missouri Press
Columbia · Missouri

To the most significant people in my life:
my mother and father, Lillian, Niki, John,
Burt, and Frank

PREFACE

THE PROBLEM OF FREE WILL is one of the most discussed philosophical problems. Its prevalence, to a large extent, is based on the fact that it involves ethical and legal questions that affect the personal life of man.

Among philosophers, the problem of determinism and freedom and its implications for moral responsibility and punishment have precipitated numerous discussions in contemporary philosophy.

The Institute of Philosophy at New York University discussed determinism and freedom in an age of science at the annual meeting in 1957. At a philosophy conference at the University of Rochester in May, 1964, all the papers read were concerned with various aspects of the problem of freedom.

In the last few years a number of controversies have developed in the philosophical journals related to the traditional problem of free will. The emphasis in this volume will be placed on the analysis of the positions of the soft and hard determinists and on the attempt to solve the problem of whether freedom is compatible or incompatible with determinism.

I am grateful to Dr. Marvin Zimmerman of the State University of New York at Buffalo and to Professor Edward Walter of the University of Missouri at Kansas City for their helpful comments. I wish also to thank Mrs. D. J. Sherman for typing the manuscript.

E. D'A.

University of Missouri—Kansas City
January, 1968

CONTENTS

CHAPTER I

INTRODUCTION

༜

IS MAN REALLY FREE? One of the perennial problems of philosophy has been the problem of free will. If everything is determined by antecedent conditions, how can we consider man's actions to be free? Is the belief that everything is determined incompatible with the concept of freedom? If all actions are determined, how can we hold an individual morally responsible or punish him for his acts? These are some of the questions philosophers have asked when examining the problem of free will.

There are four possible positions that can be taken in the free will controversy. First, the belief that determinism is false and freedom is true. This position is sometimes known as *libertarianism*. Second, the belief that both determinism and freedom are true; determinism is compatible with the notion of freedom. This position is usually known as *soft determinism*. Third, the belief that determinism is true and freedom is false. This is the position of the *hard determinist*. Fourth, the belief that both determinism and freedom are false. In the history of the controversy over free will no attempt has been made to justify this last position. Since these positions either accept or reject the notion of determinism, let us briefly examine the concept of determinism.

1

DETERMINISM

What is determinism? Determinism has been defined in various ways. Some laymen and philosophers equate determinism with fatalism. To say that everything is determined means that all events are beyond our control and that they will occur in a fixed manner, regardless of what we do.

Moritz Schlick maintains that when a scientist uses the term *determinism,* "he means that his differential equations (his laws) enable him to *calculate* E, if C and the boundary conditions are known to him. Determination therefore means Possibility of Calculation, *and nothing else.*"[1]

Mario Bunge claims that a general definition of determinism includes the principle of productivity and the principle of lawfulness.[2] All events develop out of pre-existing conditions, and they occur in definite ways that are lawful and not arbitrary. This definition of determinism allows for causal, mechanical, statistical, teleological, and other kinds of determination.

In the context of the controversy over free will, determinism is equated with the concepts of causation and predictability. Determinism, in this sense, is the view that every event has a cause and is in principle predictable. What does it mean to say that every event in the universe has a cause? This statement means that for every event in the universe there is a set of conditions such that, if the conditions C are fulfilled, the event E invariably occurs; if the same antecedent conditions should be present in the future, the same event would occur. No other event will occur, given these exact conditions. What does it mean to say that every event in the universe is in principle predictable? It means that if we knew the antecedent conditions of any event, we could predict what event would occur. It is this sense of determinism that the libertarians, soft determinists, and hard determinists use when they discuss the problem of free will.

According to this sense of determinism, all human actions are the results of hereditary and environmental influences. It is believed that, given an adequate knowledge of all the factors acting upon an individual, we could predict how he would behave under certain conditions.

In opposition to determinism, the indeterminist states that not all events are the result of antecedent conditions. No knowledge of an individual's previous actions or character can enable us to always predict how he will behave in a given set of circumstances. The indeterminist points out that we cannot predict certain events. The reason we cannot always predict certain events is not due to our lack of knowledge, but to a genuine indeterminism in nature itself. The indeterminist agrees that ninety-nine one-hundredths of a person's life might be due to heredity and environment, but, if there were a hundredth part that was not determined, that fraction would be sufficient to justify indeterminism.

In recent times, some physicists have supported indeterminism because of certain facts related to the behavior of electrons. Arthur Eddington maintains that, as a result of the advent of quantum theory, theoretical physics can no longer utilize the concept of determinism. "Determinism has dropped out altogether in the latest formulation of theoretical physics, and it is at least open to doubt whether it will be brought back."[3]

In classical physics it makes sense to say that a particle at any given moment has a definite position and a definite velocity. It is assumed that both of these factors can be conjointly known. Given the knowledge of the relative positions and velocities of a system of particles at any one moment, it is possible to calculate precisely their relative positions and velocities at any moment.

In quantum physics it does not make sense to say that a particle at any given moment has a definite position and a definite velocity at any single moment. The process of ascertaining the position of an electron alters the velocity of the electron. Conversely, the process of ascertaining the velocity of an electron alters the position of the electron. The more accurately either of these factors is measured, the greater becomes the uncertainty with respect to the other. We are unable, therefore, to predict the behavior of individual electrons.

Can we infer from the fact that we cannot predict the behavior of individual electrons that this inability is due to the indeterminate character of nature? In dealing with this problem, it is important not to make the mistake Eddington and other physicists have made in "supposing that uncertainty relations show there is anything indeterminate in Nature, or that science has now had to become inaccurate."[4] The fact that one cannot predict a particular event does not prove that this event is due to the indeterminate character of nature. It is possible that in the future we will be capable of predicting the behavior of individual electrons. It is always conceivable that further investigation will enable us to predict a particular event that at one time was not predictable. The history of science is filled with many examples of this point. A. J. Ayer claims:

> . . . it is necessary to distinguish between a disbelief in the utility of deterministic concepts and a disbelief in the regularity of sensible occurrences. For the fact that it is found convenient not to assign determinism to the "entities of reason," which are postulated as a means of describing and predicting the course of sensible phenomena, is not a proof that there cannot be universal correlations in the field of phenomena themselves.[5]

How do we justify the belief that every event in the universe has a cause? The determinist maintains that as we examine nature we find that many events have causes. It is true that in some investigations we have not discovered the causes of certain events. But the fact that these causes are difficult to find does not mean that they do not exist. We have succeeded in finding the causes of certain events and the determinist believes that we will find the causes of certain other events in the future. The determinist's thesis is that even if we never find the causes of certain events the causes nevertheless do exist.

The indeterminist denies that every event in the universe has a cause. The indeterminist would agree that we have found causes for many events in the universe, but not for all events. It is conceivable that there are events that are uncaused. The notion of an event entails the idea of something happening, not the idea of what caused it to occur. There is nothing contradictory in the belief that some events are uncaused. Fred Hoyle has shown that this belief is not only logically possible, but that on the basis of the theory of continuous spontaneous creation of matter, certain laws can be mathematically formulated to explain the emergence of certain phenomena out of nothing.[6]

The determinist maintains that the fact we have not discovered the cause of a particular event does not mean it has no cause. The area of events known to be caused constantly increases as scientists discover more causes. There is no area of events known not to be caused. There is merely an area of events not known to be caused. Therefore, we cannot say that a particular event has no cause, but only that we have not found the particular cause of that event. It is always conceivable that further investigation will reveal that an event is caused. The determinist claims that the causal principle can never be disproved.

It has been maintained that if you cannot disprove determinism, neither can you prove that determinism is true on the basis of experience. Determinism cannot be proved by experience, since we have not observed all events. Even if we could observe all present events, we could not observe certain past events as well as future events. All we can say on the basis of experience is that we find many events do have causes. We cannot empirically justify the belief that every event has a cause.

Some philosophers have contended that determinism is neither true nor false, because it is not a statement about the world. The causal principle is a leading principle of scientific investigation. It is not a description of the world, but merely a means of seeking uniformities in the world. "The causal principle is not a statement of fact about the world, it is something we bring to the world; . . . it is more like a demand or a hope we put to the world."[7]

Although determinism cannot be empirically justified, justification has been offered on the grounds that determinism is the basic presupposition of intelligent inquiry. When a particular event occurs, it is necessary to refer to its causes in order to understand why this particular event occurred. To understand any phenomenon, it is necessary to study the conditions under which the phenomenon existed.

> Determinism in one form or another is the theoretical presupposition of all intelligent activity. No social regulation could be undertaken without the assumption that human behavior is largely influenced by certain factors revealed through a consideration of man's past.[8]

When we hold a person morally responsible for his actions, we assume the validity of determinism. If an act were uncaused, then it would be a matter of chance. Under such conditions, can we hold an individual morally responsible for his acts? A man cannot be held morally responsible for his actions if they were spontaneous in the sense of being uncaused by him. Therefore, the notion of moral responsibility assumes the validity of determinism.

LIBERTARIANISM

The libertarian believes that the concept of freedom is incompatible with the concept of determinism. Since man is

sometimes considered free to act in alternative ways, libertarians deny the validity of determinism.

Charles A. Campbell is the foremost libertarian of the
twentieth century. Campbell agrees that the causal principle
operates throughout most of nature, but he contends that
certain types of human actions are not subject to causal laws.
For Campbell, an act is free in the sense required for moral
responsibility if the person is the sole cause of the act and if
he could have acted in alternative ways. "If entities other
than the self have also a causal influence upon the act, then
the act is not one for which we can say without qualification
that the *self* is morally responsible."[9]

Campbell argues that if an individual's choices are caused
by his heredity and environment, then it is a fiction that an
act is solely determined by the "self." Campbell denies the
belief that all human actions and decisions are caused by an
individual's heredity and environment. It is in this sense
that he denies the validity of determinism. He points out
that a free act is not an uncaused act, but rather an act
caused by the "self" as distinct from the "character" of an
individual. Campbell uses the phrase "contra-causal freedom" in order to express what he means by a free act: "A
contra-causal freedom . . . posits a breach of causal continuity between a man's character and his conduct."[10]

Why do human beings believe in "an indissoluble core of
purely *self*-originated activity which even heredity and environment are powerless to affect? . . . They do so, at bottom,
because they feel certain of the existence of such activity
from the immediate practical experience of themselves."[11]
Campbell claims that introspection reveals that in situations
of moral temptation the self decides whether to follow our
inclinations or to exert the effort needed to act in accordance with our sense of duty. He argues further that introspection reveals to all people who experience this kind of
moral conflict, that they can act in alternative ways, and that
their decision to act is determined solely by the self.[12]

"When we decide to exert moral effort to resist a temptation, we feel quite certain that we *could* withhold the effort; just as, if we decide to withhold the effort and yield to our desires, we feel quite certain that we *could* exert it."[13] Campbell agrees that the conviction may be a delusion, but he contends that at this moment he is not concerned with this problem.

Campbell states that in most situations our character determines our choices. But freedom exists only in those situations of moral temptation where the self decides to act in accordance with our concept of duty or to follow our inclinations. In all other situations the problem of freedom is totally inapplicable. Campbell's concept of freedom is based on his distinction between man's self and his character. "The 'nature' of the self comprehends, but is not without remainder reducible to, its 'character'; it must . . . be taken as including *also* the authentic creative power of fashioning and re-fashioning 'character.' "[14] Campbell maintains that our character determines our desires and, partly, the nature of the situation in which our decision takes place. But it does not determine the decision itself when we must decide between following our inclinations or acting in accordance with our sense of duty. This act of decision can oppose and transcend one's formed character. Therefore, the character and the self are not identical.

Campbell agrees that from the standpoint of an external observer the concept of self is unintelligible and has no meaning. He asserts that there is no reason to accept this limitation when we are considering a subjective activity, and he claims we should appeal to our inner experience. From this standpoint the notion of self is meaningful.[15] Campbell states that from an inner standpoint it is meaningful to say an act is caused by a person's self and not by his character.

> But if the self is thus conscious here of *combating* his formed
> character, he surely cannot possibly suppose that the act, al-

though his own act, *issues from* his formed character? I submit, therefore, that the self knows very well indeed—from the inner standpoint—what is meant by an act which is the self's act and which nevertheless does not follow from the self's character.[16]

P. H. Nowell-Smith says that the dispute between determinists and libertarians is largely a dispute about method, that is, the method of introspection and the method of logical analysis. Libertarians resort to introspection to justify the belief in contra-causal freedom, whereas determinists use the method of logical analysis to evaluate the reliability of introspection and to determine in what sense we are free.[17]

Campbell appeals to introspection as a means of justifying his belief in contra-causal freedom. He maintains that all people who experience a certain kind of moral conflict are aware of contra-causal freedom. It does not follow that because all people believe something, what they believe is true. All men in the past may have believed the earth was flat. The fact that a belief is universal does not necessarily mean that it is true.

Nowell-Smith states that contra-causal freedom is not something of which one could be directly aware. "If anything is certain in this obscure subject, it is that the statement 'X entails a breach in causal continuity' could not be established or refuted in introspection."[18] He maintains that the belief in contra-causal freedom may be true, but it is not self-evident. The belief in contra-causal freedom presupposes a complex mass of psychological theory that may be false, and it introduces certain terms like "self" and "self-determined" that require special rules to specify what they mean.[19]

Nowell-Smith points out that "the universal negative form of statement ('Nothing caused my decision', 'No one could have predicted my decision') does not seem to be a proper vehicle for anything that one could be said to *observe* in self-examination."[20]

The notion of contra-causal freedom is the belief that certain decisions are not caused by hereditary or environmental factors. How would a libertarian answer the determinist who claims he does not discover by introspection that certain decisions are not caused by his heredity or environment? In order to resolve this problem the libertarian must go beyond introspection and produce an argument. If the libertarian attempts to justify the belief in contra-causal freedom by the use of arguments, then he is admitting that introspection is inadequate as a means of proving his belief.

We know how to settle empirical disputes, but it is difficult to know how we can settle introspective disputes.

> There seems to be nothing available even remotely resembling the elaborate system of checks and precautions that the laboratory experimenter demands for the successful conduct of his experiments. Nor is it possible, in this sort of case, to call in a third party to review, check or repeat the experiment, for clearly no one can either verify or falsify the private introspected findings of another.[21]

R. D. Bradley maintains that we can never observe that our decisions in certain cases are not caused by our character. Not discovering the causes for certain of our decisions is not the same as knowing that our decisions are not caused by certain factors. Bradley states that "we may, under certain conditions, be able to observe X, but we can never be completely sure that we have observed non-X: it is always possible that we have instead merely not-observed X."[22] Bradley denies that our consciousness reveals the truth of such propositions as "My will is contra-causally free" and "The self has a power of absolute spontaneity," first because "the data of introspection do not in fact include *any* propositions, and, secondly, because such propositions cannot even be said to report such data, let alone report them correctly."[23]

In an appendix to *On Selfhood and Godhood,* Campbell

responds to Nowell-Smith's criticisms of his position. "What I have insisted upon is that introspection provides highly important evidence for the settlement of the question, not that it can *per se* settle it."[24] Campbell agrees with Nowell-Smith that we cannot know introspectively that we are contra-causally free. Campbell asserts, "what I report as discerned in introspection is . . . not a contra-causal activity, but a *belief*—seemingly ineradicable—that one is contra-causally active."[25] Campbell claims that metaphysics, science, epistemology, ethics, and religion can all contribute something to the justification of the belief in contra-causal freedom, but, unfortunately, he does not show how they can contribute positive evidence to support that belief. I doubt whether an appeal to these various disciplines can justify the belief in contra-causal freedom. The question still remains whether the belief in contra-causal freedom is true or false.

Campbell agrees with Bradley's criticism that propositions cannot be included in the data of introspection. But he feels that this does not affect his position. "But of course what we observe in introspection, for me, is not 'an interruption of the causal order', but a *belief* that one is bringing about such an interruption."[26] Campbell maintains that introspection does not establish a negative existential proposition, but rather the positive existential proposition: "I am the only cause of this decision."[27] The proposition "I am the only cause of this decision" is not sufficient to justify the belief in contra-causal freedom. This proposition as stated is ambiguous. It may refer to the fact that I, as a specific person with a given character, am the cause of this decision, not some other person. In order to deny the meaning of this particular proposition, Campbell must resort to asserting certain negative propositions. In affirming that "I" refers to the self and *not* to the character of a person and that the self is *not* affected by hereditary and environmental influences, Campbell is asserting certain negative propositions. Campbell's discussion of self and how it differs from the character of an individual utilizes certain negative propositions.

Campbell's position is based upon the belief in contra-causal freedom. While Campbell admits that the belief may be illusory, he claims the onus of proof rests upon those who reject this belief.[28] On the contrary, the onus of proof rests upon Campbell, who asserts this belief is true. Campbell's critics are not necessarily denying the belief in contra-causal freedom, but rather they find it difficult to accept this belief because of a lack of positive evidence. The onus of proof rests upon those who affirm a belief and not upon those who doubt it.

Since some beliefs derived from introspection have been found to be illusory or false, it is perfectly reasonable to request some evidence that the belief in contra-causal freedom is not an illusion. There are many people who have beliefs derived from introspection that have no basis in reality. Keith Lehrer maintains that

> to argue that because an experience may be deceptive it does not provide adequate evidence for accepting a hypothesis is to be committed to the untenable position that no *inductive* evidence is adequate evidence for accepting any hypothesis, for we may be deceived if we accept any hypothesis on any inductive evidence; that is, the hypothesis that we accept on the basis of the evidence may be false.[29]

Lehrer believes we have as good a reason for accepting a belief in free will based on introspection as we have for believing there is a physical world.[30]

I grant that we can be deceived about the inductive evidence for a particular hypothesis. But the scientific method is a method that enables us to repeat an experiment and to evaluate the evidence. This provides us with a method that enables us to check our results under controlled conditions. The method of science provides us with an objective method of determining when we have been deceived and of correcting our mistakes. Beliefs derived from introspection are unreliable. They are unreliable, not because they may be deceptive, but because there is no objective method of determining whether or not they are deceptive. The introspective method does not provide us with a means of evaluating our beliefs or of checking for possible deceptions.

The concept of the physical world is ambiguous. In sense one, the physical world is the name we give to an unobservable entity or substance that causes us to have certain sensations. In sense two, the physical world is the name we give to all actual and possible perceptions. I agree with Lehrer that we have just as good a reason for accepting a belief in free will based on introspection as we have for believing in a physical world in sense one. In both cases, these beliefs are unverifiable. On the other hand, the belief in free will based on introspection is different from the belief in the physical world in sense two. The belief in the physical world in sense two is verifiable, whereas the belief in free will based on introspection is unverifiable.

One of Campbell's arguments is that we must appeal to our "inner experience" in order to discover contra-causal freedom. Does introspection reveal to us a reason to believe in contra-causal freedom? John King-Farlow maintains that the prospect of settling the dispute about what introspection reveals to us is rather dim, since there have been widely divergent accounts of the findings of introspection among philosophers. "Some of these would call Campbell's appeal superficial and fallacious, others would call it superfluous, since they 'find' that consciousness can behold itself in *all* contexts, with due application, as pure freedom."[31] John Stuart Mill claims introspection reveals that he could have chosen another course of action, if he had preferred it. It does not tell him that he could have chosen one course while he preferred the other.[32] Friedrich Paulsen states that his consciousness informs him "that I am not moved from without like a cogwheel in a machine."[33] Moritz Schlick asserts that "the consciousness of freedom . . . is the knowledge of having acted of one's *own* desires."[34] Since the inner experiences of philosophers have varied, we cannot utilize their conclusions to justify the belief in contra-causal freedom.

Campbell's position also rests on the distinction between the self and the character. Nowell-Smith maintains that it is difficult to construe Campbell's position "in such a way that the 'self' can be distinguished from the 'character' without lapsing into indeterminism."[35] Campbell denies that all actions are caused by man's character and that free acts are chance or random acts that are uncaused. In this sense he denies the validity of both determinism and indeterminism. Campbell states that in situations of moral temptation man's actions are contra-causal or self-determined. A self-determined act is one caused by the self, and, therefore, it is not an uncaused act. Nowell-Smith asserts that "if 'self-determined' is to mean 'determined by the self' it is necessary to give some account of what the 'self' is."[36]

For Campbell, the self is not an event caused by other events. The self is the cause of certain acts. But what is the cause of the self? If the self is not caused by some event, then it is either uncaused or self-caused. If the self is uncaused, then Campbell's position reduces to a type of indeterminism. The other alternative is that the self is self-caused. What does it mean to say that anything is self-caused? A necessary condition of a cause is that it exists prior in time to an effect. If the self were self-caused, then it would exist prior to its own existence. This is manifestly impossible. It is logically impossible for anything to be self-caused. Richard Taylor believes that the concept of the self

> involves an extraordinary conception of causation, according to which something that is not an event can nevertheless bring about an event—a concept, that is, according to which a

"cause" can be something other than a sufficient condition; for if we say that a person is the "cause" of his act, we are not saying that he is a sufficient condition for its occurrence, since he plainly is not.[37]

Taylor points out that the concept of a self entails a notion of causality "in which things in the physical world, so far as we know, are never done or brought about."[38]

Is Campbell's concept of the self empirically verifiable? Campbell agrees that, from the standpoint of the external observer, "one can attach no meaning to an act which is the act of something we call a 'self' and yet follows from nothing in the self's character."[39] On the other hand, from the standpoint of internal experience we actually do attach meaning to the concept of the self. Campbell's argument presupposes that the meaning of a term can be derived from internal or private experience. It is doubtful that we can all agree on the meaning of self if we appeal solely to our private experiences. As we have already seen, the private experiences of philosophers have varied concerning the validity of contracausal freedom.

Campbell states that from the internal standpoint we experience the feeling that the self is capable of choosing any alternative. C. Shute points out that in situations of moral temptation we do not always feel that we could have chosen otherwise. "But the feeling of being not the victor but the vanquished in the hour of what objectively is a moral triumph, is quite possibly as common as the feeling to which Campbell refers."[40] In this situation we sometimes feel we could not have chosen otherwise. This feeling is quite common among neurotics. The internal standpoint is inadequate as a means of verifying Campbell's concept of the self and how it functions.

Campbell maintains that the self is distinct from man's character. The self comprehends man's character and has the creative power to change man's character. Campbell argues that, since the self is aware of its evaluation of the character, it cannot be derived or caused by the character. Why not? The self is the act of deciding whether to accept one's character or to change it in a situation of moral temptation. It does not necessarily follow that because man is capable of evaluating his character, the decision he makes is not caused by some aspect of his character. The fact that an individual can decide whether or not to evaluate all his decisions does not mean that this decision is not caused by some decisions he has made in the past.

A determinist would maintain that a man's character is composed of all his beliefs, values, and attitudes, as well as many other factors. All mental processes, including the decision to change his character, are part of a man's character. In this sense, the self is part of man's character and is caused by an aspect of the character or by some environmental factors. The self, that is, the decision to evaluate one's character in a situation of moral temptation, is perfectly compatible with the notion of determinism. There is no need to postulate the existence of the self in order to explain how we can decide about our decisions or how we can evaluate our evaluations. Both of these procedures can be explained within a deterministic framework without resorting to the belief in Campbell's brand of libertarianism.

Campbell's use of introspective reports as well as of the concept of contra-causal freedom does not constitute adequate evidence or argument to support libertarianism. The denial of determinism presents innumerable difficulties in justifying the notion of freedom.

CHAPTER II

SOFT DETERMINISM

ॐ

WILLIAM JAMES, in his essay "The Dilemma of Determinism," made a distinction between what he called hard and soft determinism.

> Old-fashioned determinism was what we may call hard determinism. It did not shrink from such words as fatality, bondage of the will, necessitation, and the like. Nowadays, we have a soft determinism which abhors harsh words, and repudiating fatality, necessity, and even predetermination, says that its real name is freedom.[1]

Although James rejected both hard and soft determinism, he respected the position of the hard determinist. On the other hand, he referred to soft determinism as "a quagmire of evasion under which the real issue of fact has been entirely smothered."[2] James contended that soft determinism was evasive because it had converted the free will problem from a factual and ontological problem to a verbal problem. The soft determinist maintains that the free will problem is a result of certain linguistic confusions. Once we make people aware of these confusions they will realize that there is no problem at all. The free will problem is a pseudo problem. William James rejects the soft determinist position because he asserts that the free will problem is a genuine problem

17

concerning certain questions of fact and not of words. Is William James right? Before we comment on this question, let us examine in detail the position of the soft determinist.

FREEDOM

For the soft determinist, determinism and freedom are compatible. There is no contradiction in the position that both determinism and freedom are true. An act can be both free and determined, and there is no need to deny determinism in order to affirm that we are sometimes free. To say that determinism is true is to maintain that all of our actions are caused. When I can fulfill my desires I am considered free.

According to this viewpoint, the belief that determinism and freedom are inconsistent is based on certain errors. The first error is a misunderstanding of what is implied by determinism. Determinism is equated with fatalism or with some form of compulsion. The second error is due to an incorrect analysis of *free:* Freedom is equated with indeterminism or some form of chance event. Soft determinists maintain that once we rectify these mistakes we will discover the belief in determinism to be perfectly compatible with the belief that we are sometimes free.

Determinism is not to be equated with fatalism or compulsion. Determinism usually refers to the belief that every event is determined. But *determined* is a vague term. In relation to the free will problem, *determined* sometimes means caused and sometimes has been used to mean fated or compelled. To say that every event has a cause is not the same as to say that every event is fated or compelled. There is a difference between determinism and fatalism.

A fatalist maintains that man's desires and choices are irrelevant and ineffective. All events are beyond human control, and events will occur in a predetermined way regardless of what we do. If a man is dying from lung cancer because of excessive smoking, a fatalist would maintain that no effort on the part of the individual or a physician would affect the outcome of the event. In other words, all human effort to change the course of human and natural events is futile. A fatalist is a determinist, that is, he accepts the principle that every event has a cause. On the other hand, a determinist is not necessarily a fatalist. To accept the causal principle is not to deny that people are often causal influences that help to determine whether some events will or will not occur. The soft determinist maintains that the future is sometimes determined by our effort and struggle. The stream of causation runs through our deliberations and decisions as well as through other events.[3]

The belief that determinism and freedom are incompatible is often based on equating causality with compulsion. When we say Mr. X behaved the way he did because of certain factors in his heredity and environment, we sometimes treat these factors as constraining forces that necessitated his behaving in a certain manner. Some determinists have rejected free will because they contend that all events are necessitated by antecedent conditions. What does it mean to say that causes necessitate? Since *necessitate* is an ambiguous term, it is important that we elucidate the various senses of *necessitate*.

In sense one, *necessitate* refers to a logical deduction. For example, from the premises that all men are mortal and that Socrates is a man, it logically follows that Socrates is mortal. The premises necessitate a certain conclusion. The logical sense of *necessitate* means that if we accept certain premises or antecedent conditions, it would be contradictory to deny that a certain conclusion or event will follow. Do causes necessitate in sense one? There is no logical contradiction in denying that given certain conditions a certain event will occur. Therefore, causes do not necessitate in the logical sense.

In sense two, *necessitate* refers to what we have empirically discovered concerning the nature of causal relations. When we say that Mr. X's heredity and environment necessitate this particular act, we mean we know empirically that, given these antecedent conditions, this event will probably occur. In sense two we cannot assert that an event must occur in the sense that, given certain antecedent conditions, it logically follows that a certain event will occur. This is only true with *necessitate* in sense one. In sense two, *necessitate* means it is highly probable that, given certain conditions, a particular event will follow. *Necessitate* in sense two is empirical, and, as such, can be falsified at any time by new evidence. Some determinists have erroneously interpreted *necessitate* in sense two, meaning necessary in the logical sense. Causes do necessitate in sense two, but this is compatible with the soft determinist's notion of freedom.

In sense three, *necessitate* refers to individuals being compelled by other individuals to do things against their will. If I decide to finish writing this section this evening, and I do so, my behavior is not compelled or necessitated in sense three. On the other hand, if I do not desire to finish writing this section this evening, and some individual forces me to do so, then my behavior is necessitated in sense three. Because a person acts according to his desires does not mean that his action is compelled. To say that something is compelled is to say more than just that it is caused. "All compulsion is causation, but not all causation is compulsion. Seize a man and violently force him to do something and he is compelled, also caused, to do it. But induce him to do it by giving him reasons and his doing it is caused but not compelled."[4] Causes do not necessitate in sense three, except in those cases where one person compels another person to do something that is contrary to his desires. As I will show later on, *necessitate* in sense three is incompatible with the soft determinist's notion of freedom.

The belief that events compel each other is sometimes the result of a certain animism that we accept as existing among events. "We tend to think of events as forcing each other instead of simply following each other. Perhaps we form a mental picture of an unhappy effect trying in vain to extricate itself from the clutches of an overpowering cause."[5] Hospers claims that this kind of picture-thinking gives an emotive meaning to *cause* or *determine* that is not present in its cognitive meaning. Some events regularly follow others, and this is what we mean when we talk about A being the cause of B. The type of picture-thinking that imagines events compelling each other is partially responsible for the belief that causality or determinism is incompatible with freedom.

Determinism is the belief that all human behavior is determined by causal or natural laws. Some determinists have interpreted this statement to mean that all human beings are compelled to behave in a particular manner because their behavior is determined by natural laws. This belief is based on the fact that when we say A is the cause of B, we mean A and B are connected by a law. The laws of nature are exceptionless empirical generalizations, and consequently they cannot be broken. Therefore, when A and B are connected by a law, the event B must occur whenever A happens.

This argument is also based upon the error of equating causality with compulsion. The error has arisen because of the ambiguity of the term *law*. It is assumed that all actions subject to laws are compulsory. The mistake lies in the failure to distinguish two different kinds of law: one that compels, and another that does not. There are prescriptive laws, such as the laws of the state, which prescribe how its citizens ought to behave. The state compels its citizens to obey certain laws by imposing certain threats and penalties when those laws are violated. Human laws compel in the sense of prescribing what ought to be done and what ought not be done. There are also descriptive laws, such as the laws of science. These laws describe what actually happens and they do not prescribe and compel. Schlick argues that in science *law* does not prescribe how something should behave, but rather it describes how something does behave. Since scientific laws describe only what happens, we cannot say that one event compelled another event to occur.[6] In natural science it would be absurd to say that the flame compelled the iron rod to expand.

Determinism and freedom are also considered incompatible because *free* is defined as "uncaused." If a free act is considered an uncaused event, then determinism and freedom are incompatible. Since determinism asserts that every event has a cause, it cannot be consistent with a belief that some events are uncaused.

It is true we can stipulate that *free* means uncaused. Because we can arbitrarily define *free* in whatever way we desire, we can find a meaning that is incompatible with determinism. Of course, we can also arbitrarily define *free* so that it is compatible with determinism. Ayer points out that if we give *freedom* any meaning we desire, we can always find a meaning of *freedom* that is compatible with determinism.[7] The soft determinist contends we can never resolve the free will problem if we merely stipulate whatever definition of *free* we desire. We must look for a reportive definition of *free* in contrast to stipulative definitions of *free*. We can find a reportive definition of *free* if we examine how the term is used in ordinary usage. The soft determinist claims that in ordinary usage *free* means uncompelled and not uncaused. A man claims that he is free to marry his girl, drink a glass of beer, walk down the stairs, go to the movies, go to sleep, and perform many other activities. In all these cases the man will grant that his actions were caused, but he will still maintain that he was free. He was free because no individual compelled him to perform any of these actions. "To say that free acts are uncompelled acts, then, is to give a true reportive definition of 'free', and to say that they are uncaused acts is to give a false reportive definition."[8]

Freedom is to be contrasted with compulsion and not with causality. While it is true that all compelled acts are caused, it is not the case that all caused events are compelled. If I desire to get up and walk around or to stop writing, I am free in so far as I can fulfill these desires. On the other hand, I am not free if I am subjected to some form of external constraint that prevents me from acting according to my desires. Schlick maintains that a man is free if he is able to act in accordance with his desires, and he is not free if he is compelled by outside forces to act contrary to his natural desires. Man is not free if he is chained to a rock, or if someone forces him at the point of a gun to do something contrary to what he desires.[9] The soft determinist maintains that our desires, choices, and decisions act as causes of some events that will occur. When my desires and choices cease to be causal factors in my behavior and I am compelled to do what another person wants me to do, then I am not free.

The soft determinist claims that the traditional free will problem can be resolved if we do not confuse determinism with fatalism, causality with compulsion, and freedom with indeterminism. If we adopt the meaning of *free* as employed in ordinary usage, that is, uncompelled, then determinism is compatible with freedom. Both determinism and freedom are true.

Before we turn to the soft determinist position concerning moral responsibility and punishment, let us examine some of the more fundamental criticisms that have been made of the soft determinist position concerning the nature of freedom.

Criticisms

Can we justify the definition of *free* as meaning uncompelled on the grounds that it is employed in ordinary usage? Some philosophers have attempted to use a paradigm case in order to defend this particular use of *free* as well as others. "Since the meaning of 'his own free will' can be taught by reference to such paradigm cases as that in which a man, under no social pressures, marries the girl he wants to marry . . . it cannot be right, on any grounds whatsoever, to say that no one ever acts of his own free will."[10] In regard to the paradigm case, Hardie asserts that from "the fact that 'of his own free will' has a standard use, and therefore an application, it follows that it is trivial to assert and absurd to deny that men will freely, that the will is free."[11]

MacIntyre contends that a person could be under a post-hypnotic suggestion and yet fulfill all of the conditions of a paradigm case of *acting freely*.[12] But we would not say that a person acting from a posthypnotic suggestion was acting freely. There are also other cases of people who are under no external pressure and who weigh alternatives, and yet are not considered to act freely. A person who has been drugged and a kleptomaniac are not behaving because of an external compulsion, and they do sometimes weigh alternatives. Therefore the paradigm case is inadequate, since it would require us to accept some acts as free that, in fact, are not considered to be free. The paradigm case of *acting freely* seems to be somewhat like a definition that is too broad. It includes within the area of free things those things which we do not consider to be free. Soft determinists have attempted to meet these objections by making certain distinctions, such as inside and outside factors, voluntary and involuntary, and choosing and not choosing. Whether such distinctions enable the soft determinist to meet these objections will be examined later in this chapter. Since a paradigm case can only point to a situation that is considered free, it is inadequate to meet any objections that demand that certain distinctions be made and that certain criteria be formulated to distinguish between free and unfree acts.

Ayer maintains that if we analyze *free* or *freedom* in the ordinary sense, we will discover that it is not to be contrasted with causality, but rather with compulsion. According to ordinary usage of *free* or *freedom*, I would not be acting freely if someone compelled me to do something against my will.[13] There is no denying that we sometimes use *free* to mean uncompelled, but how do we determine that this is what we ordinarily mean by *free?* The soft determinist claims that his definition of *free* is a reportive definition and not a stipulative one. But the soft determinist has not justified this claim. No empirical study has been performed to determine what is "common usage, as determined by mass observation, statistics, medians, standard deviations, and the rest of the apparatus."[14]

The soft determinist's definition of *free* seems to be one of a number of common definitions of *free*. The following are some other prevalent definitions of *free*. A free act is one that is the result of rational considerations, whereas an act is not free if it is a result of irrational factors. Closely related to this definition of *free* is the notion that an intelligent act is free and a nonintelligent act is not free. Some people use *free* in relation to alternatives existing in a given situation, and others have used *free* in direct proportion to an individual's ability to change his behavior. The soft determinist is using a more common definition of *free* than has been used by many philosophers.

Ayer has maintained that we should appeal to ordinary usage because if we do not, one could arbitrarily define *freedom* so that it would either be compatible or incompatible with determinism. R. C. Perry contends that the same thing is true about defining *determinism*. We can define *determinism* in such a way that it is either compatible or incompatible with freedom.[15] If by *determinism* we mean that all events are compelled by internal and external factors, then determinism is incompatible with the soft determinist's concept of freedom. On the other hand, if by *determinism* we mean that every event has a cause, then this is compatible with the soft determinist's concept of freedom. The soft determinist has appealed to ordinary usage in defining *free*. But has the soft determinist appealed to ordinary usage in defining *determinism?* The meaning of *determinism* in ordinary usage is not clear. Many people have no idea of what it means and others seem to equate determinism with fatalism. The definition of *determinism* in terms of the causal principle does not seem to be a common meaning of *determinism* among laymen. The question of whether or not the soft determinist's concept of determinism is derived from ordinary usage is in one way irrelevant, since there is no dispute about the meaning of determinism between the soft and hard determinists.

What is the relationship between the development of the behavioral sciences and ordinary usage? Rollo Handy claims:

> in the usual course of events, the general public will lag behind the sciences. Because the psychologist regards as determined an action which ordinary people regard as free hardly invalidates psychology. If common usage lags behind science, so much the worse for common usage.[16]

Handy demonstrates that the social setting of a particular culture determines what we ordinarily think are free and responsible acts. That these acts are so determined is a limitation. It is also true that someone who is unaware of certain developments in the behavioral sciences may very well use *free* according to ordinary usage, and yet he can be mistaken.[17] Consequently, one who relies upon ordinary usage may possess a rather unreflective and uneducated understanding of which acts are free and which acts are not free.

The soft determinist contends that the belief that determinism and freedom are incompatible has arisen in part because of the ambiguity of *law*. Schlick maintained that only legal laws constrain or compel, whereas descriptive laws merely describe relationships between events. Descriptive or natural laws do not compel or constrain anyone.

H. Fain claims that Schlick's distinction between prescriptive and descriptive laws does not adequately analyze the problem of constraint.[18] Fain believes the crucial distinction between prescriptive and descriptive laws is not that the former are passed by lawmakers and the latter are not, but that prescriptive laws can be violated and descriptive laws cannot. Laws constrain if they can be violated and never constrain if they cannot be violated. By definition, a natural law cannot be violated, whereas a prescriptive law remains a law even when it is violated. "It is not, however, because a law may be violated that it constrains behavior, as the argument seems to suggest."[19] Fain maintains that the fact that descriptive laws do not constrain does not imply that descriptive laws cannot be used to determine when certain human actions are constrained. We can state, by means of a descriptive law, the conditions under which a person will act compulsively. For example, given certain conditions Mr. X will steal any item of woman's apparel in a department store regardless of whether a clerk is watching him or whether a policeman is at his side. Schlick's analysis of prescriptive and descriptive laws does not seem to adequately explain the difference between compelled and uncompelled acts.

That human acts are compelled and that they are predictable are two entirely different facts, according to Schlick. We confuse compulsion and predictability because we sometimes use *compulsion* as a metaphor when we refer to scientific laws. "In proving that scientific laws do not compel, that predictability is not the same as coercion, he [Schlick] thinks he is proving that there is no antithesis between freedom and predictability. . . . He eliminates not the problem itself, but the *language* of the problem."[20] M. Cranston maintains that the traditional problem of freedom still remains if we change the language of the problem. He agrees with Schlick that it is inappropriate to ask whether our acts are subject to or free from scientific laws. Cranston contends that the problem of freedom remains if we reword it, and he asks whether all our choices and decisions are in principle predictable.

The problem of whether our choices are in principle predictable is not a verbal dispute, but rather a genuine one between the libertarian and the determinist. Schlick's distinction between compulsion and predictability is not made to resolve the conflict between the libertarian and the determinist, but is addressed to those philosophers who are in the determinist camp. He is pointing out that determinism entails predictability and not compulsion. Cranston has mistakenly assumed that Schlick's distinction between compulsion and predictability is being used to obscure the dispute between libertarians and determinists.

The soft determinist maintains that our actions are free if they are voluntary and not free if they are involuntary. But what is meant by *voluntary* and *involuntary?*

> The meaning is that we choose to perform certain actions and having chosen, do perform them. . . . This is a voluntary action. Wherever choice doesn't occur or, as in the case of sudden unexpected paralysis, temporary or more permanent, the chosen action doesn't come off, there is no voluntary action.[21]

This definition of *voluntary* is inadequate. We perform many acts that are not a result of a choice and yet are still considered free and voluntary. The act of walking down a flight of stairs in most cases does not involve a choice of taking one step and then another. The act of walking, as well as other habitual acts, does not always involve a conscious choice, and yet it is still considered free. There are also acts that are performed as a result of a sudden outburst of feeling. The act of warmly greeting an old friend that I have not seen in many years is not the result of a choice to act in this manner. Many nondeliberating acts are usually considered free and yet do not satisfy the above criteria of voluntary acts.

Hospers points out that if we accept the criterion of choice as a defining characteristic of a free and voluntary act, then many compelled acts would be considered free. "When a person submits to the command of an armed bandit, he may do so voluntarily in every one of the above senses: he may do so as a result of choice, even of deliberation, and he could have avoided doing it by willing not to—he could, instead, have refused and been shot."[22]

Are there cases in which an individual's behavior is voluntary and yet is compelled? That depends on how we define *voluntary*. In one sense a voluntary act is by definition an uncompelled act. For example, when an individual says he voluntarily joined an organization, he means that his act was uncompelled. No individual compelled him to join this organization. In this sense an involuntary act is a compelled act. In another sense a voluntary act is an act we choose to perform. Since choices can be compelled or uncompelled, it follows that voluntary acts can be compelled. The choice made by an individual acting under a posthypnotic suggestion is compelled because the man could not have acted contrary to what was desired or intended by the hypnotist. The behavior of the kleptomaniac is also voluntary, since he chooses to steal. But his behavior is compulsive or constrained when he has the urge to steal regardless of the circumstances of the situation. Since some voluntary acts are compelled, some soft determinists have maintained that in order for an act to be free, it must be voluntary and uncompelled.

Certain situations do occur in which it may be difficult to determine if an act is compelled. If a man is tied to a tree and he cannot escape to fulfill a certain desire, his behavior is compelled. He could not have acted otherwise. This is a clear case of compelled behavior. Whether a kleptomaniac or a man acting as a result of a posthypnotic suggestion is acting compulsively depends on the situation. If a kleptoma-

niac steals, or if a person carries out a posthypnotic suggestion, regardless of the circumstances, their behavior is
compulsive. They could not have acted otherwise. In some
cases their behavior can be controlled. A kleptomaniac
sometimes will not steal if a policeman is watching him, and
a man acting as a result of a posthypnotic suggestion sometimes will act contrary to the wishes of the hypnotist, if the
consequences of the act conflict with his ultimate values. In
both cases "reality factors" play a role in controlling the
behavior of these individuals. In contrast, reality factors
have no effect in controlling the behavior of an insane person. In this sense, the insane person's behavior is compelled
because he could not have acted otherwise. In the case of
other types of behavior it is sometimes difficult to ascertain
whether an individual is acting compulsively or the degree
to which his acts are compulsive, for example, in neurotic
behavior. It seems to me that the soft determinist needs to
analyze further the different types of compulsion and to establish a set of criteria of distinguishing compelled acts from
uncompelled acts. A system of degrees of freedom, based on
the nature of the compulsion, may need to be established.

Ayer maintains that free acts are uncompelled and that
unfree acts are compelled, and it is a mistake to equate causality with compulsion. Ayer asserts that when an act is
caused "there is an invariable concomitance between the two
classes of events; but there is no compulsion, in any but a
metaphorical sense."[23] R. C. Perry agrees with Ayer that if
we stay on a linguistic level, the relation between constraint
and causality holds. To transfer necessity from language to
fact would involve a logical contradiction. Necessity has only
a metaphorical meaning when applied to the actual world.
Perry argues that Ayer is inconsistent, since he uses *necessity*
or *compulsion* to describe the relationship among certain
events, that is, one man compels another man to do something against his will.[24] Perry is mistaken. Ayer would be

inconsistent if *compulsion* were used to describe the relationship between two events. Ayer is not saying that the gun
pointing at a man's head (cause) compels a certain type of
behavior (effect). *Compulsion* is not a descriptive term
when we are talking about the relationship among events.
But this does not mean that it cannot function descriptively
when we are explaining a certain relationship among men.
When one man forces another man to do something he does
not desire to do, we can call this a description of a compelled
act. A cause does not compel an effect, but on the human
level we call certain cause and effect relations compelled
acts. In other words, *compulsion* does not refer to the causal
relation itself, but rather it is the name we give to certain
acts that are outcomes of particular causal relations.

Paul Edwards claims that an action is free if it comes from
an unimpeded rational desire on the part of the individual;
this is how we distinguish a kleptomaniac from a thief. Edwards asserts that:

> if a rich kleptomaniac steals an article he does not need, he is
> not a free agent, because the desire from which he is acting is
> not rational. But if I go into a restaurant and order a steak
> . . . because I desire to eat a juicy, tender and nourishing
> steak, my action is free. I am acting in accordance with an
> unimpeded rational desire.[25]

Edwards realizes that *rational desire* is difficult to define. But
he claims this does not interfere with our ability to distinguish between desires which are rational and those which are
not rational. In one sense a rational desire is impossible.
Desires are not rational, but rather only people and some
animals possess rationality. I assume what Edwards means by
rational desire is a desire that we deliberate about and in
which we are concerned with the consequences of the desire.
If we accept Edwards' criteria of a free act, then many acts
usually considered free would not be free. There are many
noncompelled human acts in which deliberation and a con-

cern for consequences do not take place. Edwards is equating freedom with rational behavior. "But a free act need not be reflective, for it might be impulsive. . . . there is no contradiction in saying that a man on a particular occasion acted freely, responsibly, and on impulse."[26] I will show later that the distinction between the thief and the kleptomaniac cannot be justified by using Edwards' criteria.

If our desires have been conditioned by certain factors in society, can they be considered free? K. J. Scott maintains that although constraint is opposed to freedom, conditioning is not opposed to freedom. "Conditioned conduct not only is not constrained conduct but does not feel like constrained conduct."[27] Scott's argument is that conditioning is a form of control that does not involve constraint. With constraint we are yielding to a threat and we feel frustrated because we cannot fulfill our desires. This does not take place in conditioning. Conditioning is a form of determination, but it is not constraint.

It seems to me that the distinction between conditioning and constraint is vague. Many conditioned acts seem to fulfill the conditions of constraint. A neurotic who has been conditioned to distrust all women sometimes feels frustrated when he cannot fulfill his desires to trust his wife. Conditioned acts can be just as frustrating as constrained acts. Yielding to a threat is not only a condition of a constrained act, but also functions in some conditioned acts. A child can be conditioned by certain threats so that as an adult he behaves in accordance with these threats. A threat acts as a present compulsion in a constrained act, whereas it sometimes functions as a past compulsion in a conditioned act. ". . . there is little effective difference between a dog's refusing to go into a car because someone inside is threatening him with a whip (present compulsion) and his refusing because every time he tried to take a ride in the past he had been whipped (past compulsion)."[28] If some conditioned acts function as past compulsions and constrained acts function as present compulsions, then it is inaccurate to call the former free and the latter unfree.

John Wilson develops and examines a position similar to Scott's. Wilson asserts that a free act is one caused from within and an unfree act is one caused from outside the person.[29] How do we determine whether an act is due to an internal or an external cause?

One of the difficulties of attempting to distinguish internal causes from external causes is that many causes that seem to be internal are really external. A person may feel that the cause is within him and be ignorant or unaware of the fact that the cause is outside him. A person who does X because of a posthypnotic suggestion feels that the cause is within him; he is unaware of the fact that the cause is outside him.

One of the difficulties of using internal and external causes as a means of determining free and unfree acts is that human actions are not exclusively caused by internal or external causes. When we examine human acts we always find some causal factors in the situation that are outside of the individual. Philippa Foot claims that the view that some acts originate solely from internal causes is due to the ambiguity of the expression "caused by my desires or character."[30] The soft determinist uses this expression to mean, I can do what I desire. But this does not mean that my desire was the only factor or a sufficient condition for doing X. My desire to do X can be a cause, but this does not negate the fact that other causal factors outside of me are also operating in this situation. "Since all men, in the ultimate analysis, are entirely the products of heredity and environment, it must be admitted that if we trace the causes for their actions sufficiently far back, we shall always arrive at outside causes."[31] In other words, internal causes are actually the result of external causes.

In our discussion of conditioned and compelled acts, we

discovered that some conditioned acts can be just as constraining as compelled acts. The distinction between internal and external has little value when we are concerned with free and constrained acts. Internal causes can be just as constraining as external causes. The behavior of a person who has a compulsive obsession is just as constrained as the behavior of a person who is physically forced to do something against his will.

Ayer recognized that there exist not only external constraints, but also internal constraints. He attempts to define free and unfree acts by distinguishing internal constrained acts from internal nonconstrained acts. When deliberations cease to be causal factors in one's behavior, the behavior is constrained. When deliberations do function as causal factors, the behavior is nonconstrained. To illustrate the difference between constrained and nonconstrained behavior, Ayer refers to the kleptomaniac and the thief. "A kleptomaniac . . . does not go through any process of deciding whether or not to steal. Or rather, if he does go through such a process, it is irrelevant to his behavior. Whatever he resolved to do, he would steal all the same. And it is this that distinguishes him from the ordinary thief."[32]

Ayer is maintaining that the kleptomaniac does not deliberate, or if he does, it does not make any difference in his behavior. His behavior is compulsive in the sense that he would steal regardless of the consequences. This compulsion is why his behavior is constrained. It is interesting to note that authorities in psychology and criminology maintain that the kleptomaniac does not exhibit the behavior as stated by Ayer and other philosophers.

Although kleptomania is sometimes referred to as compulsive stealing, the kleptomaniac's behavior possesses "different qualities and dynamics from compulsive actions."[33] Dr. Donald Cressey, a criminologist at the University of California at Los Angeles, doubts that there is an irresistible impulse to

steal in most cases of kleptomania.[34] "The strongest kleptomaniac urge can probably be momentarily controlled while
the person knows he is being watched. 'The policeman at
the elbow test' which some courts have employed for irresistible impulse would permit very few diagnoses of irresistible
impulse."[35] The "policeman at the elbow test" means that
the individual who committed the crime would have done so
even though a policeman had been standing beside him. F.
Alexander and H. Staub maintain that while the impulse in
kleptomania is unconscious, the act itself is not completely
unconscious, as is generally the case with compulsive behavior.[36] The evidence indicates that Ayer is mistaken in believing a kleptomaniac's behavior is compulsive in the sense that
he is acting as the result of an irresistible impulse.

Cressey contends that kleptomaniacs are motivated in the
same way that thieves are motivated. "They select secluded
places in which to perpetrate their acts, plan their activities
in advance, realize that they will be arrested if detected, and
do many other things indicative that there is a conscious
normative referent in their behavior."[37] Kleptomaniacs deliberate, they are somewhat aware of their behavior, and
they will not steal if they are being watched by a clerk or a
policeman. The evidence does not invalidate Ayer's position,
but it does show that we can no longer use the kleptomaniac
and the thief to illustrate the difference between a constrained and a nonconstrained act. Ayer would have been
wiser to have selected a compulsive act for which there is
empirical confirmation.

We see that Ayer's criterion of deliberation as a defining
characteristic of a free and nonconstrained act is unsatisfac-
tory. There are many nondeliberating acts which are nonconstrained. If we accepted Ayer's criterion, then habitual
acts and acts of impulse would be considered constrained
acts. The act of brushing one's teeth would be considered a
constrained act.

The difficulty with defining *free* and *not free* by using such criteria as voluntary and involuntary, internal and external, conditioned and constrained, compelled and uncompelled, is that these criteria are vague. The soft determinist maintains that the sufficient condition for an act to be free is that the act be voluntary and uncompelled. Since we can point to certain cases in which a man's actions are voluntary and not compelled by internal and external causes, then some acts are free. The fact that it is difficult to classify some acts as being compelled or uncompelled does not negate the fact that some acts do satisfy these conditions.

MORAL RESPONSIBILITY

The soft determinist claims not only that determinism is compatible with freedom, but that determinism is compatible with moral responsibility and punishment. Determinism is compatible with a corrective view of blame and punishment. We blame and punish people because we believe that blame and punishment function as causal or determining factors in modifying the behavior of certain individuals. The soft determinist rejects a retributive justification for blame and punishment and accepts a deterrent and reformative basis for blaming and punishing certain individuals. Let us examine the views of some soft determinists who claim that determinism is compatible with moral responsibility and punishment. The views of Moritz Schlick and Nowell-Smith will be critically examined.

According to Moritz Schlick, our interest in determining whether someone is responsible for a particular act is based upon determining who is to be punished for this act. The meaning of punishment lies in its creation of certain causes and motives of conduct that will affect human behavior. "Punishment is an educative measure, and as such, is a means to the formation of motives, which are in part to prevent the wrongdoer from repeating the act (reformation) and in part to prevent others from committing a similar act (intimidation)."[38]

The question concerning who is responsible for a particular act is, for Schlick, the same as the question concerning who is to be punished for this act. Determining who is to be punished depends upon whether an individual's motives can be altered by punitive means. If a man is punished, then in similar situations in the future the altered motives will cause him to refrain from repeating this particular action.

Schlick maintains that the question of who is responsible should not be interpreted to mean we are trying to discover who is ultimately responsible for this act. He grants that an individual's great-grandparents, the social milieu, and inherited factors contribute to the development of this individual's character. Schlick claims that such remote causes are irrelevant to questions concerning moral responsibility and punishment.[39]

An individual is held morally responsible if his behavior can be altered in the future by means of reward or punishment. If an individual's motives cannot be altered by means of reward and punishment, then we would not hold him morally responsible. An insane man is not morally responsible, because promises or threats would be incapable of altering his behavior. If a man is subjected to some form of external constraint, he is not held morally responsible for what he was compelled to do. We would hold morally responsible the man who forced the individual to act against his will.

A thorough analysis of Schlick's theory has been given by C. A. Campbell.[40] Campbell maintains that if we accept Schlick's theory of moral responsibility, then lower animals would be considered morally responsible for their behavior. "It is quite possible, by punishing the dog who absconds with the succulent chops designed for its master's luncheon, favorably to influence its motives in respect of its future behavior in like circumstances."[41] Since punishment or the threat of punishment can alter or modify a dog's behavior, a dog is considered morally responsible. This is consistent with Schlick's view that moral responsibility is to be attributed to those who can be effectively punished. But we do not consider dogs morally responsible for their acts. Therefore, Schlick's notion of moral responsibility is inadequate on this point.

Does the case of the dog parallel that of the man? The dog does not reason or know the difference between right and wrong, whereas a man does reason and knows the difference between right and wrong. This is why a man is held morally responsible and a dog is not held responsible. It seems to me that Schlick cannot use these distinctions between a man and a dog because for him moral responsibility is determined by effectiveness of punishment and not by other factors. The distinction between the man and the dog is irrelevant to Schlick's conception of moral responsibility. For Schlick, the only reason that a man is morally responsible is that his behavior can be modified by means of punishment. Since a dog's behavior can also be modified by punitive means, he also must be held morally responsible.

Sidney Hook proposes a similar argument in response to Campbell's criticism of Schlick's concept of moral responsibility:

> We blame children more as they approach the age of rationality . . . because the growth of intelligence enhances the subtlety, range, and effectiveness of their choice. And if animals could think or respond to reasons, we would blame them too, because we could build up within them a sense of blame, shame, and responsibility.[42]

Hook is equating blame with the degree of rationality. This concept of blame is probably more consistent with how we actually attribute moral responsibility, but it is a deviation from Schlick's conception of moral responsibility. Schlick does not consider the degree of rationality, or any other factors except the effectiveness of punishment, as a means of determining moral responsibility.

People sometimes speak of someone who is dead as being morally responsible for a particular event in the present. For example, Hitler is often blamed and held morally responsible not only for the murder of millions of Jews, but also for the attitude that some Germans have about Jewish people. Can we hold Hitler morally responsible for this situation if we accept Schlick's concept of punishment?

> Clearly we cannot now favorably affect the dead man's motives. No doubt they could at one time have been favorably affected. But that cannot be relevant to our judgment of responsibility if, as Schlick insists, the question of who is responsible "is a matter only of knowing who is to be punished or rewarded."[43]

But we do blame people and hold them morally responsible even though they are dead and inaccessible to any type of punitive action. Therefore, Schlick's concept of moral responsibility is inadequate in that it would not enable us to blame certain people who are no longer living.

Schlick's concept of moral responsibility in relation to blaming dead people can be justified. If by blaming dead people we are implying they were capable of being affected by punishment at the time of the act, then we can justifiably blame certain people who are no longer living. Hitler is blameworthy because he belongs to a class of individuals who are considered blameworthy, even though they are no longer living. They are blameworthy because they would have acted otherwise if they had been punished. If Hitler were insane, as some people have claimed, then he would not be considered blameworthy.

Schlick identifies the question, "Who is morally responsible?" with the question, "Who is to be punished?" Schlick claims that in ordinary language moral responsibility is equated with the deterrent or reformative type of punishment. Is it? Schlick has not substantiated his claim by any empirical survey concerning the usage of *blame* and *punishment*. Sidney Hook claims that in ordinary language *blame* is vague and inconsistent, and therefore we cannot appeal to ordinary usage in this case.[44] My experience indicates that certain retributive elements are present in the layman's conception of punishment. Schlick's contention, that in ordinary language moral responsibility is equated with deterrent or reformative punishment, is implausible.

P. H. Nowell-Smith maintains that an individual is morally responsible if his behavior can be altered in the future by means of praise and blame. Nowell-Smith illustrates his position by referring to a schoolmaster who has two pupils who have failed to solve a certain problem in arithmetic:

> The schoolmaster knows from experience that, if he adds the fear of punishment to the motives actuating A, then A will tend to get these sums right in the future, which is, for him, the end to be achieved. On the other hand, if B is stupid, neither threats nor promises will cause him to do better.[45]

Nowell-Smith contends that this is why we hold a thief morally responsible but do not hold a kleptomaniac morally responsible. "The reason is that we believe that the fear of punishment will affect the future behavior of the thief but not that of a kleptomaniac."[46]

Only those acts that can be altered by means of praise and blame or rewards and punishment are considered moral. Rewards and punishments are distributed, not because they are deserved, but because they are useful in altering the behavior of some individuals.

Nowell-Smith claims that the class of acts that can be altered by means of punishment is identical with the class of acts that are voluntary. If an act can be altered by punitive means, it is a voluntary and moral act, and the individual who committed the act is considered to be responsible for it. A person is not considered morally responsible for committing a certain act if he was compelled to do so by another individual. He is not considered responsible because punishing him would not prevent the same event from occurring in the future.

It seems to me that Nowell-Smith's concept of moral responsibility omits some basic factors of how we actually justify blame and punishment. Nowell-Smith has stated the necessary, but not the sufficient, condition of moral responsibility.

Can blame and punishment be justified solely by their effects and not by other factors? M. Mandelbaum argues that praise and blame are not merely justified by their effects, but rather we praise someone because we think his action is right and we blame someone because we think his action is wrong. "The future conduct of those we praise and blame . . . is purely coincidental."[47] The justification of punishment is partially based upon the fact that a law has been broken. Responsibility and punishment are appropriate when a moral rule has been violated, not simply because punishment is an effective means of modifying behavior.

R. L. Franklin claims that blame might lose its effectiveness if the individual to be blamed knew its purpose was to influence his behavior. If the individual ignored the prospect of blame in the future because of its attempt to influence his behavior, then the blame would cease to be effective. There "are unfortunately men who act on the set and deliberate policy that moral criticism is to be sneered at or ignored when it conflicts with their chosen aims."[48] These men are unamenable to praise and blame, and yet they are sometimes considered morally responsible for their actions.

Nowell-Smith's theory is inadequate, since his definition of responsibility and punishment is too broad. His definition would include many things that we do not consider to be blameworthy or punishable. D. D. Raphael contends that if we accept Nowell-Smith's theory, "we shall have to widen the class of voluntary and morally responsible behavior far beyond the limits in fact observed in the ordinary use of language."[49] Franklin claims that we know some power-drunk tyrants and cold-blooded gangsters are not amenable to moral pressures, yet no one would exculpate them from blame.[50]

Cranston maintains that, since "blame and punishment *does not* affect the behavior of the hardened criminal, the hardened criminal cannot be said to be morally responsible for his misdeeds."[51] If we accept Nowell-Smith's theory, we cannot blame a hardened criminal no matter what crime he performs. We do, however, blame a hardened criminal, even though he cannot be reformed. Hook maintains that when people blame a hardened criminal who cannot be reformed, they are not blaming him for the latest action, but rather for a whole set of criminal acts that he has performed.[52] Hook's explanation of why we blame a hardened criminal may be plausible, but Nowell-Smith cannot use it. Nowell-Smith justifies blame in terms of its effectiveness in modifying behavior, and Hook's concept of blaming a hardened criminal is not concerned with modifying human behavior at all.

If we accept Nowell-Smith's position, then we accept response to praise as a necessary condition for being considered praiseworthy. But a man may be completely indifferent to praise and yet be considered praiseworthy. Jean-Paul Sartre rejected the praise of those who awarded him the Nobel Prize, yet he can still be considered praiseworthy for his contributions to the field of literature.

J. D. Mabbott criticizes Nowell-Smith's view that an act is moral if it is inducible by punishment, and it is not moral if it is not inducible by punishment. "My ability to write legibly is not a moral trait, yet it was certainly induced by punishment."[53] Nowell-Smith's definition of "moral" is too broad. It would necessitate calling many acts moral that we do not consider to be moral.

Nowell-Smith's concept of moral responsibility assumes the validity of the utilitarian theory of punishment. The justification of punishment is that it will deter or reform the behavior of an individual.

By the deterrent effect of punishment is meant the effect on others of making them abstain from undesirable acts simply for fear of punishment. The threat of punishment probably does operate as a deterrent in some cases. To what extent does it operate as a means of curbing the behavior of different types of people? Is it an effective means of changing behavior? What are the consequences of this theory of punishment?

The deterrent principle of punishment is based on the hedonistic assumption that people regulate their behavior by calculation of pleasure and pain. According to this assumption, if the pain of the penalty overweighs the pleasures to be gained by the crime, the individual will usually not commit the crime. If punishment effectively deterred crime in this way, how can one explain that criminals do exist? The fact that criminals do exist shows that criminals usually do not consider the penalty for a particular crime they commit. Sometimes they are acting on the basis of a psychological disturbance, or they are acting under the stress of a great emotion. H. Munsterberg points out that the threat of punishment will be ineffective in situations where a child considers the criminal a hero, and where jail is just one of many inconveniences an individual experiences in his slum life.[54] The threat of punishment is ineffective in many instances because the factors motivating human behavior are not affected by the threat of punishment.

The ineffectiveness of punishment as a deterrent can be observed in the numerous violations made by ordinary citizens. Parking and speeding regulations, as well as other laws, are continually being broken. G. Aschaffenburg points out that at the moment a crime is decided upon, the idea of punishment has very little effect as a countermotive. The criminal works on the assumption that he will not get caught, therefore he looks at the penalty merely as a remote possibility.[55]

The ineffectiveness of punishment as a deterrent can also be seen in the high rate of recidivism among criminals. (A recidivist is an individual who has been convicted of a crime after having been convicted of a previous crime.)

Some people have claimed that the death penalty is an effective deterrent. A study by K. F. Schuessler has shown that the death penalty does not effectively deter crime.[56] Schuessler tested the deterrent influence of the death penalty in states that have abolished capital punishment, by comparing the homicide rates before and after the abolition. This comparison showed that the states that abolished the death penalty had no unusual increase in the homicide rates. Some of these states restored the death penalty after a few years on the grounds that the murder rate had increased after the abolition. The statistics show that increases in homicide rates were almost parallel in other states that made no changes in their laws regarding the death penalty. A comparison of the homicide rates of several European countries before and after each abolished the death penalty shows that the existence of the death penalty has no perceptible effect on the incidence of murder. "Belgium . . . where no capital punishment has been carried out for years, has also had no increase of the crimes for which capital punishment is the penalty."[57]

What are the effects of the deterrent principle? A. C. Ewing claims that punishment inflicted as a deterrent will tend in the direction of gross cruelty.[58] The more painful the punishment, the more a deterrent is the punishment likely to be. Since no punishment succeeds in deterring everybody from committing a crime, there are always grounds for making punishment more severe in order to increase the number deterred by it. Ewing states that if we accept the deterrent principle, the severity of the punishment ought not to be decreased because the temptation to commit a crime was strong. The deterrent principle suggests that punishment should be increased, since the stronger the temptation the greater must be the punishment needed to deter the crime.

The deterrent notion of punishment is definitely limited in the extent of its effectiveness. It seems to have more disadvantages than advantages in its application.

With the reformative theory of punishment, the reform of the individual is the sole end and justification of punishment. The theory assumes that punishment tends to reform people. The following illustration has been given to support this belief: If a number of bees swarm out of their hive and sting the boy who molests them, they will not be troubled by him in the future.

A painful experience, such as being punished or being stung by bees, may make an individual think twice before repeating an act. But the fact that an individual has been made more cautious by the previous suffering does not necessarily mean that he has been reformed. Ewing contends that, since pain or the fear of pain is a nonmoral motive, it cannot bring about moral improvement.[59] If a criminal abstains from future crimes because he has suffered for them in the past, his motive is not a moral one. Since his motive is a fear of suffering, his character is basically unchanged. In other words, he refrains from acting in a certain way because of the fear of punishment, and not because his character has been reformed. If the fear of punishment was removed, he would probably commit the same crime again.

The theory assumes that punishment brings about repentance and reform. Punishment, by its infliction of pain and privation, may in certain cases bring about the reform of the individual. I contend that such cases are the exception rather than the rule, and that the reformative value of punishment has been greatly exaggerated. In this connection it is significant that pain, as such, has a corrosive effect on the moral character of an individual. Punishment often embitters the criminal, and thereby fosters the very antisocial tendencies that it was designed to eradicate.

There is a psychological factor that detracts from the reformatory value of punishment. The fear of pain and its correlative, the desire for pleasure, are not the main springs of human actions. Their function is auxiliary. They reinforce and exhibit our drives, but they are relatively impotent.[60] Therefore, the fear of future pain is powerless to curb an immediately compelling impulse. Moreover, the memory of pain is notoriously short-lived. Pains that seem almost unbearable as they are experienced fade rapidly in remembered intensity as they recede into the past. Try to conjure up in your memory the most intense pain of your life, and you will find it surprisingly lacking in vividness.

The failure of punishment, especially in the form of a prison sentence, to bring about reform may be explained by an interesting trick of memory. An interval of time that may seem long in passing, shrinks enormously in retrospect. "In general a time filled with varied and interesting experiences seems short in passing, but long as we look back. On the other hand, a tract of time empty of experiences seems long in passing, but in retrospect short."[61] What better explanation is there for the ineffectiveness of punishment as an instrument of reform?

The reformative principle of punishment used as a means for improvement has a number of unanticipated consequences. Punishment often isolates the individual who is punished and makes him a confirmed enemy of the group or of society. When the sole reaction is punitive, criminals are isolated from law-abiding groups and neither understand nor are understood by these groups.

K. G. Armstrong points out that if we accept the reformative theory, then "every sentence ought to be indeterminate—'You stole a loaf of bread? Well, we'll have to reform you, even if it takes the rest of your life.' From the moment he is found guilty the criminal loses his rights as a human being quite as definitely as if he had been declared insane."[62] The criminal does not lose his rights as a human being, but he loses his rights as a citizen to live in society and to engage in everyday activities. Armstrong's equation of a criminal with an insane person is inadequate. Some criminologists maintain that insane persons and criminals are the same, in the sense that both are to be treated and not punished. But the fact that they are both treated does not mean that the nature and causes of their behavior are similar. The reformative theory of punishment does not uphold that every sentence should be indeterminate. Armstrong has confused the reformative theory of punishment with the reformative theory of treatment. The basis for the indeterminate sentence is that one cannot intelligently determine how long it will take to rehabilitate a criminal independently of examining him, his background and problems, and many other factors. I doubt that it would take a lifetime to rehabilitate a person who stole a loaf of bread.

This analysis has shown that there is very little evidence that punishment effectively deters or reforms the behavior of an individual. It is unsound to base a concept of moral responsibility on the validity of the deterrent and reformative theories of punishment.

The soft determinist can still justifiably hold certain people morally responsible for their actions. If an act is considered to be free, then the individual who performed the act is morally responsible.

Chapter III

HARD DETERMINISM

ೠ

THE SOFT DETERMINIST CONTENDS that determinism is compatible with freedom and moral responsibility. In contrast, the hard determinist maintains that determinism is incompatible with the concepts of free choice and moral responsibility. The hard determinist criticizes the soft determinist for not pursuing his analysis far enough. The soft determinist arbitrarily stops his analysis of the problem at the desires or choices that are the cause of some of our actions. The hard determinist asserts that this is a shortsighted view of the entire problem; we must continue our analysis and inquire as to the causes of our desires and choices. If we trace the chain of causes back far enough, we will discover that ultimately our desires and choices are caused by factors outside of our control. If we look at the problem from a farsighted position, we will see that determinism is incompatible with the notion of freedom and moral responsibility.

In contemporary philosophy, the hard determinist's position has been defended by Paul Edwards and John Hospers. Since there are variations in their respective positions, let us examine them independently.

THE HARD DETERMINISM OF PAUL EDWARDS

Paul Edwards agrees with William James that to a certain extent the soft determinist position is an evasion. The soft determinist's affirmation that desires and choices have causal influences upon some events is not denied by the hard determinist. Paul Edwards contends that the issue between the soft and hard determinist is not whether we can sometimes fulfill our desires and choices, but whether we can be considered free and morally responsible if our desires are caused by factors that are outside our control. If determinism is true, then ultimately "our desires and our whole character are derived from our inherited equipment and the environmental influences to which we were subjected at the beginning of our lives. It is clear that we had no hand in shaping either of these."[1]

To illustrate his argument Edwards uses an example of two people who are suffering from a particular neurosis. There is a known therapy that can cure an individual if the person has the energy and courage to undertake a certain treatment. A has the energy and courage to undertake this treatment, while B does not. A undergoes this treatment and is cured, but B just becomes more neurotic. Although A changed his character, his desire to change was already there. The energy and courage needed by A in order to undertake this therapy are due to factors that he did not create. A's desire to change is due to certain hereditary and environmental factors that he did not create.

There seems to be no dispute between the soft and hard determinist about the facts in this controversy. The soft determinist does not deny that an individual is ultimately the result of factors over which he has no control. The soft and hard determinists draw different inferences from these facts. The hard determinist infers that man is never responsible for his actions, whereas the soft determinist does not draw this inference.

Edwards claims that one can justify the inference of the hard determinist by utilizing C. A. Campbell's distinction between two conceptions of moral responsibility.[2] Campbell maintains that the ordinary unreflective person who is ignorant of advancements in science will consider an individual morally responsible if his behavior was not compelled. If his behavior is in accordance with his desires, he is considered morally responsible. If his behavior was compelled, then he is not considered morally responsible. The fact that a man's desires are ultimately due to factors outside his control is not sufficient reason to consider this individual not morally responsible. The soft determinist does not consider this fact to be sufficient reason to deny man's moral responsibility, whereas the hard determinist does consider this fact to be a sufficient reason to deny that man is ever morally responsible. Campbell points out that a reflective person adopts a different conception of moral responsibility. He requires not only that a person's behavior be uncompelled, but that the individual could have chosen otherwise under these circumstances.

Edwards interprets the reflective sense of moral responsibility to include not only that an individual's behavior is uncompelled, but "that the agent *originally chose his own character*—the character that now displays itself in his choices and desires and efforts."[3] Campbell contends that determinism is compatible with the unreflective sense of moral responsibility, but that it is incompatible with the reflective sense of moral responsibility.

Edwards accepts Campbell's analysis of moral responsibility, except for certain qualifications. He does not agree that unreflective and uneducated people use one concept of moral responsibility and reflective people use another concept of moral responsibility. He maintains that the same person in one context or situation will employ the unreflective sense of moral responsibility and in another situation will employ the reflective sense of moral responsibility. Edwards maintains that everyone employs the unreflective conception of moral responsibility when their judgments are based on emotive factors, such as hate or anger. In contrast many people, whether they are educated or not, employ the reflective concept of moral responsibility "when they are judging a situation calmly and reflectively and when the fact that the agent did not ultimately shape his own character has been vividly brought to their attention."[4] Edwards points out that Clarence Darrow appealed to the reflective sense of moral responsibility in convincing jurors who were somewhat uneducated.

Edwards asserts that, in analyzing these two concepts of moral responsibility, only one of them can be considered a moral concept. "Confining myself to judgments, I would say that a judgment was 'moral' only if it was formulated in a calm and reflective mood, or at least if it is supported in a calm and reflective state of mind."[5] A judgment of moral responsibility based on violent emotions or simply upon a positive or negative feeling is not considered moral. Edwards maintains that the reflective sense of moral responsibility is the only sense that can be considered a moral concept.

In a footnote to his article, Edwards states that he hopes to present a fuller treatment of the problem and to meet the criticisms of his position in the near future. Unfortunately, he has never developed his paper further or responded to his critics. Let us now turn to the criticisms that have been made of Edwards' brand of hard determinism.

Criticisms

Arthur Danto disagrees with the position that a judgment is moral if it is formulated in a calm and reflective mood. "But this is at best a necessary condition: Himmler was the most dispassionate of men, and was prepared to cite the best science he knew to back his administration of justice."[6]

Danto is implying that a reflective and calm mood is not a sufficient condition for calling a judgment moral. There are many judgments that are made in an impersonal and reflective manner that are not moral judgments. It seems to me that the validity of Danto's argument depends on what he means by *moral*. Unfortunately, Danto does not say how he is using *moral* in this context. Edwards could respond by stating that by definition a judgment is moral if it is uttered in an impersonal and reflective manner. But would this be a stipulative definition of *moral?* If we examine the way the word is used in our language, it becomes obvious that there are uses of *moral* that are not equivalent to Edwards' definition. The history of ethical theory shows that there are moral philosophies that define *good* and *moral* in terms of the subjective feelings of an individual. In fact, the emotivists have shown that certain uses of *good* are equivalent to certain expressions of likes or dislikes.

Edwards is involved in a curious kind of spurious reasoning in this particular argument. He adopts Campbell's distinction between the unreflective and the reflective senses of moral responsibility and adds that the reflective sense is the only moral concept because it is made in a calm and reflective state of mind. This view implies that the unreflective sense of moral responsibility is not a moral concept, since it is not made in a calm and reflective manner. But the unreflective sense of moral responsibility is the sense used by the soft determinist in classifying voluntary and uncompelled acts as morally responsible. There is no evidence that this classification is made in an emotive and unreflective manner. In fact, there are cases of people who employ the reflective sense of moral responsibility in an emotive and unreflective manner. There are some people who find it psychologically satisfying, because of their past experience, to accept the notion that we are never morally responsible because we did not ultimately create our own character, regardless of what the arguments or evidence may be in this dispute.

Edwards assumes that because the name of the category is "reflective" the people who employ this concept of moral responsibility are using a reflective procedure. The reflective sense of moral responsibility refers to the position that we are not morally responsible because our choices are ultimately caused by factors outside our control. The procedures used to arrive at this conclusion are not necessarily reflective rather than emotional. Edwards' contention that the reflective sense of moral responsibility is the only one that qualifies as being moral, since it is used in a calm and reflective manner, is not supportable by the available evidence. Edwards' argument is self-defeating. If we accepted his reasoning, the unreflective sense of moral responsibility would qualify as being moral when judgments are made in a calm and reflective way.

Sidney Hook maintains that the hard determinist's concept of moral responsibility is vacuous and meaningless. There are no possible conditions under which an individual can be considered morally responsible. Since *moral responsibility* has no intelligible opposite, it is cognitively meaningless.[7] But is it the case that *moral responsibility* has no intelligible opposite? Edwards suggests that man would be considered morally responsible if he originally chose his own character. Hook contends that this definition of moral responsibility is obscure:

> Since every decision to shape or choose one's character, to be responsible, must be one's own, and therefore already an indication of the kind of person one is, the notion that one can ultimately and completely shape or choose one's character is unintelligible.[8]

It is interesting to note that John Hospers, who also defends hard determinism, maintains that Edwards' position is self-contradictory:

> To cause my original make-up, I must first have existed, and to exist I must already *have* some "original make-up." I can't cause myself unless I'm already there to do the causing. . . .

> To choose a character, we must already *have* a character. Being the cause of our own original make-up is, we see, a self-contradictory notion.[9]

Hospers points out that it is a *non sequitur* to conclude that we are never morally responsible because we are not the cause of our original character or make-up. He agrees with Hook that "the cause of our original character" does not describe any actual or possible situation.

I agree with Hook and Hospers that "the cause of our original character" is unintelligible and self-contradictory. But Edwards' position can be modified to meet these objections. Instead of saying that moral responsibility is dependent upon man choosing his original character, one can say that moral responsibility is dependent upon man choosing his character. It seems to me that, whereas "choosing one's original character" is self-contradictory and unintelligible, "choosing one's character" is not self-contradictory and can be made intelligible. What possible state of affairs does "choosing one's character" describe? It is possible that, in the future, man will be able to go to a factory and choose a different body than he now possesses. In the same way he may be able to specify what kind of personality or character he desires and go through a process of immediate transformation. In this sense "choosing one's character" is just as intelligible as "choosing a suit" or "choosing a particular kind of hair-cut."

Some hard determinists, including Edwards, may not accept this modification as a sufficient condition of moral responsibility. It can be argued that the choice to adopt a new character is part of my old character. The choice itself can be traced back to certain hereditary and environmental influences that I did not create and over which I had no control. In this sense, no one would be morally responsible, even if he could change his character.

If the hard determinist's notion of moral responsibility

has no intelligible opposite, then one cannot make distinctions between who is and who is not morally responsible. Danto states that certain distinctions must always be made concerning who is responsible. When we contrast babies and men, there is a sense in which men are responsible and babies are not responsible.[10] In one sense, Danto is correct. There is a sense in which men are responsible and babies are not responsible. If we use the degree of rationality as the basis for determining who is to blame, then Danto is correct. A hard determinist recognizes the difference between babies and men in the sense that men are much more rational than babies. But it does not follow that, because we recognize this distinction, we must hold one morally responsible and the other not morally responsible. For the hard determinist the basis of determining who is morally responsible is not dependent upon the degree of rationality, but whether the acts of a person are due ultimately to factors outside of the individual's control. Danto's criticism is based on using a different standard in order to determine who is morally responsible. But a hard determinist is not committed to use Danto's standard.

Danto goes on to say: "Edwards, I think, exploits the fact that we do recognize excusing conditions, and then tries to force an analogy between an excusing condition and any condition, so that every causal explanation of human behavior immediately qualifies as an excuse."[11] From the perspective of a soft determinist, a person's behavior is excusable if it has been compelled, and it is inexcusable if it has been uncompelled. The fact that a causal explanation can be given for both a compelled and an uncompelled act does not mean that both are excusable. Danto's argument is based on the point of view of the soft determinist. But Edwards' position is based on a different perspective. It is obvious that if Edwards employed the perspective of the soft determinist, he would not be a hard determinist. From Edwards' perspective, a causal explanation of an act would qualify it as being excusable, since it implies that the causal sequence ultimately refers to factors outside of the individual. If we assume that all acts have a causal explanation (that determinism is true), then all acts are excusable from the perspective of the hard determinist.

Richard Brandt states that

> the distinction between excusable and inexcusable misbehavior cannot be abandoned altogether. It is necessary for a desirable system of criminal law, . . . in overt moral criticism, and perhaps in the private moral thinking and feelings of mankind, irrespective of the truth of determinism.[12]

Howard W. Hintz agrees with Brandt and adds that a social order is not possible if we do not recognize excusing conditions in our everyday experiences.[13]

Brandt and Hintz's argument is based on the assumption that social order, criminal laws, and moral evaluation cannot exist unless we distinguish and recognize the difference between excusable and inexcusable behavior. This is an unfounded assumption. I can easily imagine a society where social order, criminal law, and moral evaluation exist, and yet no attempt is made to classify acts as being excusable and inexcusable. A criminal can be distinguished from a noncriminal in the sense that one does not obey the laws of the state and the other does obey the laws of the state. We can make this distinction without necessarily holding the criminal or the noncriminal morally responsible. An insane person who commits a crime is a criminal, even though he is not considered morally responsible.

Some philosophers have claimed that our social order will collapse if we do not hold criminals morally responsible. A social order is threatened when the society does not protect itself against undesirable elements. But what is to prevent a society from placing a criminal in prison in order to protect its citizens? Criminologists have for many years been saying that prisons should not be punitive, but rather they should be treatment centers. The imprisonment of an individual does not necessarily mean that he is considered morally responsible. This position does not imply that it would be moral to imprison a noncriminal or a person whose behavior is compelled. A noncriminal is not imprisoned, because there is no need to modify his behavior. He has not violated the laws of the state. An individual whose behavior is compelled may or may not need to be imprisoned. If A's behavior is compelled by B, and as a result a law is violated, then it does not make sense to imprison A. It is B's behavior and not A's that needs to be changed. On the other hand, if a man has a compulsive urge to kill every woman who looks like his mother, he should be imprisoned because his behavior is undesirable and detrimental to society.

If one morally evaluates a man's behavior in terms of its effect on society, it does not necessarily follow that one must also consider him morally responsible. It seems to me that one can distinguish between a criminal and a noncriminal, a sane and an insane person, and a good and a bad act by setting up certain criteria. The validity of these distinctions is based on our criteria and not upon the added qualification that we consider some people morally responsible and others not morally responsible.

Sidney Hook contends that Edwards is inconsistent when he pleads for the innocent or condemns the guilty:

> For to be morally innocent of having committed an evil deed entails that one is not morally responsible for its commission, and to be morally guilty entails that one is. If moral responsibility is a vacuous expression, then moral innocence and guilt are too.[14]

Hook claims that the concepts of moral innocence and moral guilt entail the notion of moral responsibility. Moral innocence and moral guilt may imply moral responsibility, but there is no contradiction in asserting that certain acts are good and others are bad and also asserting that no one is morally responsible. We determine whether an act is good or bad by judging whether it conforms to a particular standard that we adopt. If we use the utilitarian standard, an act would be considered good if it produced more pleasure than pain. The fact that we deny that an individual is morally responsible does not negate the fact that this act is good according to the utilitarian standard. From the soft determinist's position it may be that moral evaluations presuppose the notion of moral responsibility. From the standpoint of hard determinism, moral evaluations can be made without presupposing the concept of moral responsibility. Edwards can condemn the act of a person because it is bad and still not hold this individual morally responsible.

A hard determinist can make moral evaluations within his own framework. Spinoza, who was a hard determinist, maintained that determinism is compatible with establishing moral values. Spinoza defined *good* as that which we know is useful to us in our attempt to realize our ideal. *Evil* is defined as that which is a hindrance to us in attaining a particular good. "Thus one and the same thing can be at the same time good, bad, and indifferent. For instance, music is good for him that is melancholy, bad for him that mourns; for him that is deaf, it is neither good nor bad."[15] In the same way, Edwards or other hard determinists can judge acts to be good or bad on the basis of adopting a certain moral standard. Hard determinism is compatible with adopting a certain standard to evaluate human behavior. In this sense, hard determinism does not destroy all prescriptive ethics.

Sidney Hook asserts that hard determinism

> leads to sentimentality, to so much pity for the criminal as a victim . . . that there is not sufficient pity or concern left for the criminal's victims—not only for his past victims but his future ones and the victims of others his actions may inspire.[16]

It is not a necessary consequence of hard determinism that it will lead to sentimentality and pity for the criminal. I grant that some hard determinists do react this way toward criminals, but so do some soft determinists. It also does not follow that because a hard determinist has pity for a criminal, he cannot have pity for the criminal's past, present, and future victims. Anyhow, what is wrong with having pity for a criminal? We often pity certain people because we realize that their hereditary and environmental influences have not been as advantageous as ours.

Hook maintains that the hard determinist's position would increase the amount of cruelty and suffering in the world and would justify the belief that everything is permissible if one can get away with it. I do not understand why the hard determinist's position would necessarily lead to an increase in the amount of cruelty and suffering. The fact that all acts are excusable and are not deserving of punishment does not necessarily mean that everything is permissible. The hard determinist can advocate that criminals should be imprisoned for the welfare of society. Prisons are not necessarily punitive. They can function as treatment centers for the rehabilitation of criminals just as asylums do in the case of insane men, who admittedly are not deserving of punishment. Hook is assuming that, since the hard determinist does not hold anyone morally responsible, he will sanction any kind of act, even if it is injurious to himself and others in our society. This assumption is not correct. A hard determinist can evaluate human behavior and take certain active steps to prevent cruelty and suffering, even though he believes that no one is morally responsible. The prevention of cruelty and suffering is dependent upon accepting certain values. This does not necessarily include the notion of moral responsibility.

Ernest Nagel argues that the hard determinist's position is irrelevant in determining who is morally responsible. Nagel points out that a baby sitter, who has certain abilities, is morally responsible for performing certain tasks. "The fact that she did not create her own body, or that she did not choose the education she received, are not relevant considerations for judging whether she is morally responsible for some event that may take place during my absence from home."[17] From the standpoint of soft determinism Nagel is correct. A person is morally responsible if he has certain capacities and if his acts are uncompelled. But Nagel's criticism of hard determinism is unfair. He is criticizing hard determinism from the perspective of soft determinism. A hard determinist does not deny that we can distinguish between a compelled and uncompelled act. However, he does not consider this to be a sufficient condition for moral responsibility.

Nagel attempts to justify his concept of moral responsibility as being sufficient by stating that this is how the notion of moral responsibility is actually used in our language. H. Van Rensselar Wilson agrees with Nagel that if a hard determinist recognizes the distinction between compelled and uncompelled acts and yet fails to consider uncompelled acts as being morally responsible, then linguistic usage is being violated.[18] To my knowledge, there has been no statistical survey to determine what is the ordinary usage of *moral responsibility*. Sidney Hook, a soft determinist, claims that in ordinary usage *blame* is vague.[19] Consequently, we cannot appeal to ordinary usage in order to justify the claims of Nagel and Van Rensselar Wilson. The soft determinist's concept of moral responsibility has a wider use in our language than the hard determinist's concept of moral responsibility. But this does not invalidate the hard determinist's position. Edwards maintains that historically it has been the hard determinist's, not the soft determinist's, conception of freedom and moral responsibility that concerned philosophers debating the problem of free will.

Van Rensselar Wilson contends that the power or nature of a choice is not diminished just because our decisions have prior causes. "Whatever moral responsibility I have for my decision, I have as their proximate cause, and the responsibility is not diminished by showing that responsible selves (as well as irresponsible selves) have causes."[20] I grant that the power of our choices is not necessarily lessened just because the choices are caused. But the hard determinist has never denied this position. The hard determinist has contended that, since our choices are ultimately caused by factors outside of us, we are not morally responsible. Similarly, the hard determinist has never denied that man is the proximate cause of his actions. Van Rensselar Wilson seems to be assuming that there are factual disagreements between the hard and soft determinists. This does not seem to be the case. The hard and soft determinists are using different definitions of *moral responsibility*. The differences between these two positions are not factual, but they seem to be linguistic.

Elizabeth Beardsley explains the differences between the positions of soft and hard determinism by using her theory of multiple moral perspectives.[21] From the perspective of moral worth, we praise and blame certain acts in terms of their relative worth. From the perspective of moral credit, we blame or praise an individual in terms of the circumstances in which his act took place. The soft determinist is justified in blaming and praising certain acts from the perspectives of moral worth and moral credit, but from the perspective of ultimate moral equality no one is morally responsible for his actions. Everyone is equal in the sense that all our acts are ultimately caused by factors outside of our control. This is the perspective from which the hard determinist looks at human actions. The difficulties between the soft and hard determinists have partly been caused by the fact that they have used different moral perspectives.

THE HARD DETERMINISM OF JOHN HOSPERS

John Hospers states that the soft determinist's conception of freedom and responsibility is inadequate because it defines freedom and responsibility solely in relation to the conscious acts of individuals. Hospers contends that if we were aware of the effect that unconscious motivation had upon our conscious and deliberate acts, we would not consider man to be free or morally responsible. Hospers also feels that the belief that an action is free if it is determined by a man's character is also inadequate. A man's character is basically formed before the age when an individual can do anything about it. "What if even the degree of will power available to him in shaping his habits and disciplining himself now to overcome the influence of his early environment is a factor over which he has no control? What are we to say of this kind of 'freedom'?"[22]

Hospers maintains that if we examine conscious and deliberate acts, we will discover it is the unconscious that determines what our conscious acts will be. In support of this thesis Hospers discusses a number of examples of conscious behavior that are motivated and determined by unconscious forces.

A woman who has been married and divorced a number of times chooses one of three possible men to marry. She may deliberate about each man and consider their individual advantages and disadvantages. But if she is a certain psychological type, she will inevitably choose the man that most resembles her previous husbands. Her attempt to justify her choice rationally is merely a camouflage of the unconscious forces that determined the choice.

> If she is a certain kind of masochistic strain, as exhibited in her previous set of symptoms, she *must* choose B: her super-ego, compels her to make the choice she does, and even to conceal the real basis of the choice behind an elaborate facade of rationalizations.[23]

Hospers points out that when a psychologist says a man's acts were compelled by unconscious conflicts, he is not using *compelled* in a literal sense. In a literal sense, a compelled act is one that is due to an external force that is imposed upon and against man's desires. When a psychologist states that a man is "compelled by unconscious conflicts to wash his hands constantly," he means "nothing can change it—it is as inevitable for him to do it as it would be if someone were forcing his hands under the tap."[24]

Hospers also uses an example of a man who is addicted to gambling, to prove that conscious acts are determined by unconscious forces. The man who is addicted to gambling spends all his money, sells his property, neglects his children, and engages in all sorts of activities in order to get money for gambling purposes. This man may deliberate about these acts and think that he is acting freely, since he consciously decides the course of his own acts. The gambler can never quit while he is winning, and consequently, in the long run, he always loses. The gambler is unaware of the unconscious factors that cause him to gamble.

Hospers claims that if we examine these cases, we will discover that the behavior of the woman and the gambler are voluntary. But their behavior is due to certain unconscious forces and is as inevitable as if someone were compelling them to behave in a certain manner. Therefore, even though their behavior is voluntary, they are not considered to be free or morally responsible. The difficulty with defining free acts as those which are voluntary is that this analysis does not go far enough.

> In a deeper sense we cannot hold the person responsible: we can hold his neurosis responsible, *but he is not responsible for his neurosis,* particularly since the age at which its onset was inevitable was an age before he could even speak.[25]

Hospers points out that what he means by *inevitable* is that, given an individual's total background, his subsequent behavior is unavoidable. Man cannot avoid his childhood experiences.

> He was subject to influences—stresses, strains, conflicts, paren-
> tal quarrels, neglect, hatred, then divorce and his mother's
> subsequent life. This series of influences, . . . inevitably led
> to his being rebellious, hating and loving the same objects,
> envious of respectability yet contemptuous of it, each influ-
> ence expressing itself in a different way.[26]

Hospers agrees with Edwards that man is not morally responsible, since his acts have been molded and shaped by
childhood experiences that he did not create and over which
he had no control.

Hospers' examples of behavior that is not free or responsible are cases of neurotic behavior. Does this mean that a
nonneurotic is free and responsible? Hospers states that, in
practice, psychoanalysts have defined freedom and responsibility in this way. A person is considered free in inverse
proportion to his neurotic behavior. In this sense there are
degrees of freedom.

Hospers does not accept the psychoanalysts' definition of
freedom and moral responsibility. From Hospers' perspective the neurotic and nonneurotic are similar in that they
did not cause their own character. He agrees that neurotics
are not responsible, since their behavior is the result of in-
fantile and unconscious conflicts that they did not create.
However, he points out that a nonneurotic character is also
the result of causes he did not create and that are outside his
control. "And if, unlike the neurotic's, his behavior is
changeable by rational considerations, and if he had the will
power to overcome the effects of an unfortunate early environment, this again is no credit to him; he is just lucky."[27] If
a person has the energy to change his behavior, then this is
no credit to him, but to his psychic legacy, which he did not
create. Some people who are strong-willed tend to blame
other people because they are weak-willed and cannot

change their behavior as readily as can those who are strong-willed. Hospers asserts that weak-willed people cannot behave the way some strong-willed people expect them to behave, since they are not psychologically constructed the way strong-willed people are constructed. "We cannot with justification blame them for their inability, any more than we can congratulate ourselves for our ability."[28] Some people can overcome their deficiencies. Hospers agrees, but he contends that these people are lucky. What does Hospers mean by *lucky?* He means that some people are fortunate in possessing the power to exert the effort necessary to change their behavior. "Some of us, luckier still, can overcome [deficiencies] with but little effort; and a few, the luckiest, haven't the deficiencies to overcome."[29] But isn't it a matter of effort and not a matter of luck? Hospers agrees that it is a matter of effort, but whether a person is capable of the necessary effort to change his behavior is a matter of luck.

If we can overcome the effects of our childhood experiences, the ability to do this is a result of our childhood environment, which we did not create. We could not have created this ability, and if we lack it, we should not be blamed for not possessing it. Those of us who have this ability are fortunate, that is, lucky.

Hospers maintains that because *free* and *responsible* are meaningful in one context does not mean that they are meaningful in another context. Hospers suggests that we operate on two levels of moral discourse. The upper level is the area of the actions themselves, and the lower level is the area of the springs of action. On this upper level we can distinguish between compelled and uncompelled, voluntary and involuntary, and responsible and nonresponsible acts. These distinctions are meaningful on this level of moral discourse.

When we examine the lower level of moral discourse, we find that the distinctions made on the upper level can no

longer be made. Hospers states that these distinctions cannot
be made, since we are ultimately the kind of people we are
because of certain factors in our childhood that we did not
create. All moral distinctions disappear on the lower level.
Hospers points out that to determine "whether or not we
have the ability to overcome deficiencies of early environment, is like the answer to the question whether or not we
shall be struck down by a dread disease: 'it's all a matter of
luck.' "[30] Hospers feels that if we keep this idea in mind, we
will be more tolerant towards other people who are unlucky
or are less fortunate than we are.

Criticisms

Sidney Hook disagrees with Hospers that, when we examine human acts, the element of ability or effort is a matter of
luck. Hook maintains:

> "It's all a matter of luck" is no more sensible than saying:
> "Nothing is a matter of luck"—assuming "luck" has a meaning
> in a world of hard determinism. It is true that we did not
> choose to be born. . . . It is not true that everything that
> happens to us is like "being struck down by a dread
> disease."[31]

Hook contends that the treatment and cure of disease would
not have begun unless we believed we could change things.
What we can change is what we are responsible for.

When Hospers says "it's all a matter of luck" he is not
referring to all causal factors. He is only referring to those
causal factors that affect our behavior and that are outside
our control. The parents we have, the culture we were raised
in, and our native abilities are factors we did not create and
over which we had no control. "Luck has to do with things
outside one's control, such as native ability and favorable
environmental circumstances."[32] In so far as we can distinguish between factors that are outside man's control and factors that are not outside man's control, *luck* does have a

meaning in a world of hard determinism. *Luck* is sometimes used in relation with chance events that are considered uncaused. *Luck,* in this sense, is incompatible with hard and soft determinism. John Hospers is not using *luck* to mean an uncaused event.

Hospers does not assert that everything that happens to us is like being struck down by a dread disease. Hospers is only referring to those things that happen to us and are outside our control. He is referring to whether or not we have personality disturbances, or whether or not we have the ability to overcome deficiencies of our early environment. I grant that being struck down by a dread disease is not always beyond our control. But those things that happen to us and are beyond our control are similar to cases in which we are struck down by a dread disease over which we have no control. I agree with Hook that the treatment and cure of disease would not have occurred unless we believed we could change things. But Hospers does not disagree with Hook on this point. Hospers would probably say we can at times change the course of events, but whether or not we have the ability to make these changes is due to childhood experiences that we did not create and over which we had no control. Hook defines responsibility in terms of what man can change. Hospers rejects this definition of *responsibility,* since the ability to change or not to change is due to certain past factors that man did not create and that were outside of his control. The differences between Hook's and Hospers' positions are not factual, but linguistic.

Howard Hintz contends that Hospers' position would destroy rationality in human experience. If a man's character is completely determined by previous conditioning, then:

> whether a man reasons or not is then completely dependent on the allegedly fortuitous and contingent factors that shaped his nature and character. His reasoning or nonreasoning then becomes pure accident and is therefore, by definition, removed from the area of rational choice.[33]

Hintz claims that Hospers' position is actually a form of fatalism, based on a number of unproved assumptions. Hintz asserts that Hospers' position is different from the soft determinist's position because there is nothing empirical about Hospers' thesis.

Does Hospers' position destroy all rationality in human experience? "We are seeking the truth at whatever cost, whether or not we like what we may find."[34] Hospers adds that even though hard determinism may be true, it would not negate the activities of blaming, praising, and being rational, since in some cases they do have a utility. The practice of being rational can be justified by its utilitarian function, regardless of the truth of hard determinism. It seems to me that Hospers' position does not imply that reasoning or nonreasoning should be removed from the area of rational choice. I am sure Hospers would agree that reasoning is more desirable than nonreasoning when we make choices. Hospers' thesis is that the ability or inability to be rational about certain matters is due to certain factors in our early environment that we did not create and could not control. A person can possess the ability to be rational about A, B, C, and D and yet not possess the ability to be rational about E. This does not negate the fact that people do possess the ability to be rational about certain matters. Therefore, Hospers' position does not negate all rationality in human experience.

Is Hospers' position a form of fatalism? That depends upon what we mean by *fatalism*. In one sense, a fatalist is one who denies that man's choices or decisions have any effect in the world. Hospers is not a fatalist in this sense. He agrees that in some instances an individual's choice does make a difference in what will happen. However, Hospers asserts that the ability to make a particular choice under given circumstances is determined by factors in our heredity and early environment. It is in this sense that Hintz consid-

ers Hospers a fatalist. If this is the case, then the soft determinist is also a fatalist. A soft determinist also believes that
we acquire our abilities as a result of hereditary and early
environmental influences. The hard and soft determinists do
not disagree about the facts, but they interpret the facts
differently. Hintz's concept of fatalism or predeterminism
seems to be equivalent to the long-range view of determinism that is recognized by both the hard and soft determinists. The long-range view of determinism maintains that if
we go back far enough in time, we will discover that all our
acts are ultimately caused by factors of heredity or environment that we did not create.

Hintz claims that Hospers' position is based upon certain
unproved assumptions. Unfortunately, Hintz does not state
what these unproved assumptions are. He also claims that
there is nothing empirical about Hospers' position. This
claim is not exactly true. Hospers does make references to
the empirical evidence of clinical psychology in support of
his position. Hospers' position does not conflict with the
claim that we do not empirically know the degree to which
the human organism can within itself overcome prior conditioning. Hospers would probably claim that an individual's
ability or inability to overcome his prior conditioning is due
to certain factors in his heredity and early environment that
he did not create. The empirical evidence concerning the
degree to which an individual can overcome prior conditioning will never refute Hospers' position. In this sense there
may be something nonempirical about Hospers' thesis.

Peter Bertocci and Richard Millard contend that although
unconscious forces sometimes affect what will happen on the
conscious level, they do not always do so. There are times in
the life of a gambler when he will not gamble. There are
intervals in the life of some neurotics when their neurosis is
discontinued for a short period of time. Bertocci and Millard
claim that a neurotic is free in those instances where his

neurosis is not affecting the choices he makes. They claim that in this sense it is not true that man is never free.[35]

Bertocci and Millard point out that a neurotic is also free in the sense that he can make certain choices within his own framework. The fact that a homosexual may have no freedom in relation to heterosexual responses does not mean that he has no freedom at all. If someone is neurotic about X, it does not mean he is neurotic about everything.

Does Hospers' brand of hard determinism undermine the search for truth? Bertocci and Millard maintain that if our deliberations and conclusions are the result of unconscious forces, there is no basis for accepting one person's conclusions over another person's conclusions.

> Indeed, why should we trust a psychoanalyst's conclusions about his patient's troubles more than the patient's? For the psychoanalyst's conclusions are not the result of an unbiased search for truth, but the consequences of the chain of events in his unconscious over which he has no rational control.[36]

Bertocci and Millard contend that Hospers' position implies that an individual's conclusions are determined by his unconscious and not by the available empirical evidence. They believe Hospers' thesis would negate the use of scientific evidence in order to determine what is true. F. S. C. Northrop agrees with Bertocci and Millard on this point:

> The question addressed to Professor Hospers is, "If all theories obtained by rigorous scientific methods are rationalizations in the vicious sense of the word, how can you be sure that the Freudian theory in which you have so much confidence—whose scientific methods still remain misty and unclarified—is not also a vicious rationalization?"[37]

Hospers would agree that we are not neurotic about everything. He does distinguish between neurotic and nonneurotic behavior. However, he would not agree with Bertocci and Millard's claim that nonneurotic behavior is free. Nonneurotic behavior is not free because, like neurotic behavior, it is the result of causes in our early environment that are outside our control. Hospers also does not deny that a neurotic can make certain choices within a particular framework. Hospers does not define freedom and moral responsibility in terms of an individual's ability to make certain choices, which is the soft determinist's concept of freedom and moral responsibility. Hospers argues that whether an individual has or has not the ability to make certain choices is due to certain causal factors in his childhood that are outside his control. Hospers recognizes the differences between neurotic and nonneurotic behavior and the ability and inability to make certain choices. But there are also similarities between these different types of behavior. They are all similar in the sense that they are ultimately caused by factors in our early environment that we did not create. These factors are why both neurotic and nonneurotic behavior are not considered free or morally responsible.

Does Hospers' position undermine the use of scientific evidence as a reliable means of arriving at true conclusions? It seems to me that Bertocci and Millard's criticism is based upon certain misunderstandings. Hospers asserts that the ability to be rational or to base certain conclusions on scientific evidence is the result of prior conditioning that is outside our control. This belief does not negate the fact that we are rational about certain things in our experience, or that we can appeal to scientific evidence to resolve certain problems. The justification of the scientific method is not dependent upon its source, but upon its consequences. The reliability of the scientific method is based upon the fact that, when we examine our past experience, we find that the scientific method is superior to faith, intuition, authority, and other methods as a means of acquiring knowledge. The pragmatic justification of the scientific method is not negated by Hospers' thesis.

Bertocci and Millard claim that we cannot trust the conclusions of a psychoanalyst because his conclusions are derived from his unconscious, over which he has no control. It is a well-known fact that all psychoanalysts undergo psychoanalysis before they start their practice. They have been supposedly cured of their neuroses before they start to deal with patients. Presumably, therefore, the psychoanalyst will not project his own neurosis on his patients, but he will be able to utilize available evidence of the causes of particular neuroses in order to treat his patients. The conclusions reached by a psychoanalyst are not derived from his unconscious. What is derived from the unconscious is the *ability* to use a rational and scientific approach. The justification of a rational and scientific approach is based upon its results, and not whether some people have the ability to apply it in certain areas.

Northrop is mistaken when he asserts that Hospers' thesis implies that all theories justified by the scientific method are rationalizations. A theory is justified as being scientific if it satisfies the conditions or criteria of a scientific theory. Some theories are rationalizations, but these theories are not scientific. A rationalization, by definition, is not scientific, since it rejects the actual evidence in attempting to justify a certain conclusion. Hospers' position does not imply that all theories are rationalizations, in the sense that the unconscious negates the ability of man to utilize a scientific approach. I agree with Northrop that some of the concepts of Freudian theory are unscientific. But this does not invalidate Hospers' position. Hospers is appealing to the empirical evidence used by psychoanalysts and other psychologists concerning the causes of neuroses and the effect our childhood experiences have on our present behavior.

Herbert Fingarette asserts that even if we accept the part that the unconscious plays in human behavior, we can still accept responsibility for our behavior.

> In spite of Hospers' assumption that we cannot be held responsible for the inevitable consequences of uncontrollable events, we seem to see in therapy an acceptance of responsibility for just such events. We also see a new way of looking at responsibility.[38]

Fingarette argues that the practice of psychoanalysis indicates we must accept responsibility for those characteristics that are the inevitable results of our childhood. An adult is no longer a child, and he must accept responsibility for the modification of his character.

> Hospers looks to antecedents of the act in order to settle responsibility. The real issue as revealed by our present perspective, however, is this: What is the (moral-therapeutic) solution to the present human predicament, granted that what happens now is a causal consequence of what happened when we could not control what happened?[39]

Fingarette agrees that neurotic adult behavior stems from childhood neuroses, but he maintains that man is still responsible in that he can decide to accept responsibility for his future acts. In other words, Fingarette is contending that we should accept responsibility for our future acts, regardless of our handicaps and limitations.

Is it true that Hospers and Fingarette really disagree? Hospers is saying we are not responsible for our neuroses. Fingarette is saying we are not responsible for our neuroses, but we should accept responsibility for our future acts. Hospers is using *responsibility* differently than Fingarette. Hospers defines *responsibility* in relation to antecedents, and Fingarette defines *responsibility* in relation to future consequences. They are using different senses of *responsibility* in their respective arguments. They are looking at the problem from different perspectives. I agree with Edward Madden that, "if this is the case then his and Fingarette's views could not conflict because they do not meet on the same ground;

yet Fingarette offers his view as a devastating criticism of Hospers'."[40] The basic difference between Hospers' and Fingarette's positions is linguistic and not factual.

The hard determinist defines *free* and *moral responsibility* differently from the way the soft determinist defines these terms. The hard determinist has a different conception as to what constitutes a sufficient condition of freedom and moral responsibility. The hard determinist also uses a different moral perspective in determining whether an individual is morally responsible.

CHAPTER IV

COULD HE HAVE ACTED OTHERWISE?

℘

SOME SOFT DETERMINISTS have claimed that additional criteria are needed in order to state the sufficient condition of freedom. In order for an act to be free, it must fulfill three conditions: The act must be voluntary, it must be uncompelled, and it must be true that the individual could have acted otherwise.

Some philosophers have claimed that determinism is incompatible with the belief that an individual could have acted otherwise. If the belief that a person could have acted otherwise is one of the criteria of a free and responsible act, then man is not free or morally responsible.

G. E. Moore contends that there is a proper and legitimate use of *could*, in which we know from human experience that some things that did not happen could have happened.[1]

What is the sense of *could* in which we know at times that we could have done what we did not in fact do? For example: What is the sense of *could* in "I could have walked a mile in twenty minutes"? According to Moore, the meaning is "I could have walked a mile in twenty minutes, if I had chosen to do so." Moore states that "We often use the phrase, 'I could,' simply and solely, as a short way of saying, 'I should, if I had chosen.' "[2]

75

When we say that something could have happened that in fact did not occur, we mean "it should have happened, if I had chosen," or, "it would have happened, if someone else had chosen." In this sense of *could*, something could have happened that in fact did not occur. These facts are consistent with determinism, namely, the principle that everything has a cause.

A similar position to Moore's has been developed by Nowell-Smith, who maintains that *could have* can be analyzed into *would have if,* because it is a suppressed hypothetical and needs an if-clause in order to complete it. Nowell-Smith claims that if one has the opportunity to run a mile, is fond of running, and has no reason for not running, then he will run. This is because "it follows that 'can' is equivalent to 'will . . . if . . .' and 'could have' to 'would have . . . if. . . .' "[3]

For Nowell-Smith, the proposition "he could have acted otherwise" is not a categorical proposition, but a hypothetical one. When we hold people morally responsible for their actions, as when we say, "he could have acted otherwise," we mean this phrase is translatable into a number of hypothetical propositions.[4]

When a husband slaps his wife and we say "he could have acted otherwise," we mean that this phrase can be translated into one or more hypothetical propositions. *He could have acted otherwise* is translatable into *he would have acted otherwise, if he had chosen.* The husband is considered morally responsible because we know that he would have acted differently if he had chosen to do so. On the other hand, if the husband was compelled to slap his wife, he would not be considered morally responsible for this act. *He could not have acted otherwise* means *he would not have acted differently, even if he had chosen or desired to do so.*

In analyzing G. E. Moore's position, J. L. Austin asks whether *could have, if I had chosen* means the same as *should have, if I had chosen.*[5] Austin maintains that *could* and *should* mean two different things.[6] What an individual could do is not the same as what he should do. Using Moore's example, "I could have run a mile, if I had chosen" and "I should have run a mile, if I had chosen" are not equivalent.

If we accept Moore's position, then if I had chosen to run a mile in twenty minutes, I should have done so. This position means that if I made a certain choice, the fact that I made this choice should cause me to run the mile in twenty minutes. But this seems to be a naive position. The running of a mile in twenty minutes occurs under certain conditions. Other conditions besides a choice to run the mile in twenty minutes are necessary in order for the event to occur. I grant that choices may sometimes be instrumental in a particular act that ensues, but from the fact that an individual makes a choice, nothing really follows except the fact that he made the choice.

Austin contends that it is wrong to say that the meaning of *I shall, if I choose* is such that my choosing to do something is sufficient to cause me to do it, or that if I choose to do something, I shall do it. This can be demonstrated by the following example: A man chooses to watch television tonight instead of reading a book. The choice of watching television is not sufficient to prove that he shall watch television. The existence of a television, good reception, and numerous other conditions are also necessary in order for this man to watch television. Not one of these conditions constitutes a sufficient condition for this man to watch television. Therefore it is erroneous to maintain that if I choose to watch television, I shall.

Nowell-Smith claims that *could have* is like *would have*. It is a suppressed hypothetical that needs the addition of an if-clause in order to complete the sentence. *Could have* is equivalent to *would have if*. Austin points out that the transition from *can* to *will* or *could* to *would* presents difficulties just as great as the transition from *could* to *should*.⁷ We know from experience that an individual may have the opportunity, the ability, and a motive for doing something and yet will not do it. A young man may have the opportunity to engage in premarital sexual intercourse with a young lady, the ability to perform the act, a motive for performing the act, but will not do it. He is a Catholic and his priest has told him it would be against God's law, and immoral, to engage in premarital sexual intercourse. It is obvious from this example that *can* is not equivalent to *will*.

Austin maintains that *could have* may be and very often is a past conditional verb. In this sense, an if-clause is needed to complete the sentence. But *could have* is often a past indicative of the verb *can*. In this sense, it is equivalent to "I was in a position to" or "I was able to," for example, "I could do it ten years ago." Austin asserts that *could* has a dual role. It sometimes has a conditional meaning and sometimes has an indicative meaning. If *could have* can function as a past indicative, it does not always need an if-clause.⁸

What conclusions can we draw from the linguistic treatment of *could have acted otherwise*? *Could have* statements are sometimes indicatives, and it is not always necessary to attach an if-clause to the statement. The statement *could have acted otherwise* cannot be ruled out as a categorical proposition. Therefore one cannot justifiably maintain that *could have acted otherwise* must always be translated into one or more hypothetical propositions. Austin has shown that there is a linguistic confirmation for the categorical interpretation of *could have acted otherwise*.

Nowell-Smith agrees with Austin that *can* is sometimes used to make categorical statements, and that *could have*, being its past indicative, is also used to make categorical statements. "The form 'could have' is often not a subjunctive, but the past indicative of 'can.' . . . It means not 'would have been able, if . . .,' but categorically 'was able.' "[9] However, Nowell-Smith maintains that it is the use of *could have* in moral contexts that is at issue and that Austin has not shown his analysis of *could have* to be relevant to the problem of freedom and moral responsibility.

When we hold people morally responsible for their actions, do hypothetical propositions adequately explain what we mean when we ask whether an individual could have acted otherwise?

We often have no doubt that a person could have acted otherwise if he had chosen or if the situation had been different. C. A. Campbell maintains that even if we were confident that a person would have acted differently, if he had chosen, this does not remove our doubts as to whether he is morally responsible for performing this particular act.[10]

Sometimes our doubts concerning a person's moral responsibility generate from certain beliefs that man's actions are, in some sense, necessitated and could not have been otherwise. To assert that a man could have acted otherwise, if the circumstances had been different, in no way negates the hardest type of determinism. One can agree that a person could have acted otherwise if he had chosen and still maintain that he could not have acted otherwise in this situation under the same circumstances. These two propositions are compatible. Richard Taylor says that the hypothetical rendition of *could have acted otherwise* is like arguing "though a man has died of decapitation . . . he could have lived on—meaning only that he would have lived had he somehow kept his head on."[11]

Nowell-Smith asserts that:

> the fallacy in this argument lies in supposing that when we say "A could have acted otherwise" we mean that A, being what he was and being placed in the circumstances in which he was placed, could have done something other than what he did. But, in fact we never do mean this.[12]

How can Nowell-Smith justify the claim that this is not what we mean? This is what Campbell means when he inquires as to whether an individual could have acted otherwise. In fact, when we examine the philosophical literature in this area we find confirmation for the categorical interpretation of *A could have acted otherwise.*

J. D. Mabbott asserts: "I remain convinced that moral responsibility requires that a man should be able to choose alternative actions, everything in the universe prior to the act, including his self, being the same."[13]

H. D. Lewis concurs with Mabbott:

> We can retain the ideas of obligation and guilt as properly ethical ideas, if we can also believe in actions which could have been otherwise than they were, even though everything else in the universe had remained the same.[14]

It remains to be seen whether the hypothetical or categorical interpretation of *A could have acted otherwise* is relevant when we consider the moral responsibility of a particular individual.

Campbell states that the hypothetical is irrelevant in our concern with whether a particular person is morally responsible for this specific action. We are concerned with a definite person with a definite character, placed in a definite set of circumstances at a definite time. A is morally responsible if he could have acted otherwise under the same conditions in which he did act. This is the categorical interpretation of *could have acted otherwise.*

> No doubt this supposititious being could have acted otherwise than the definite person A acted. But the point is that where we are reflecting, as we are supposed in this context to be reflecting, upon the question of A's moral responsibility, our interest in this supposititious being is precisely nil.[15]

It is possible that an individual could have acted otherwise if he had chosen some other alternative. But we are not interested in what he would have done if the conditions of the event had been different. We are interested in a particular man, with a definite character, placed under a definite set of circumstances, at a definite time. Now we ask the question: Could this man, at this particular time, have acted otherwise? *Could have acted otherwise*, in the categorical sense, refers to past and present time and conditions. Therefore, when we say that a man is not morally responsible for his actions or could not have acted otherwise, we are referring to a particular time and to particular conditions in the past or present. To say that a man could have acted otherwise if he had chosen otherwise refers to a set of different conditions.

For Campbell, an individual is morally responsible if he could have acted otherwise under the same conditions in which he in fact did act. If he could not have acted otherwise under the same conditions, then he is not considered morally responsible.

A judgment of moral responsibility, as Campbell has defined it, refers to a past or present event with definite conditions, and not to an event with different conditions. Even though it may be true that a person could have acted otherwise if he had chosen otherwise, this fact would be completely irrelevant to the question of whether he is morally responsible for what he actually did do.

Is it possible to prove, in the categorical sense, that an individual could have chosen otherwise?

Arthur Pap maintains that if we are aware in a given set of circumstances that we can pursue one or more courses of action, then we could have chosen otherwise. To deny that we could have chosen otherwise is to deny that we have this particular awareness. Since we are aware of alternatives, choices do exist in sense one, that is, in a psychological sense.[16]

In one sense, moral responsibility is determined by the

fact that an individual is aware of existing alternatives. In another sense, moral responsibility is concerned with acts and not with psychological states. In this second sense, when we inquire as to whether a person could have chosen otherwise we are concerned with the actual behavior that took place. It is this sense of choice that is subject to debate. The existence of the psychological sense of choice is not sufficient to prove the existence of the behavioral sense of choice. In other words, just because I feel that I can make a choice does not prove that I can in fact make a choice.

The intuitionist claims that we know we could have chosen otherwise, because we feel certain that more than one course of action was open to us when we did X. W. D. Ross contends that in considering the intuition of choice we must distinguish between the freedom to choose and the freedom to do what we have chosen.[17] Ross claims that we are only aware of the latter sort of freedom and that we are never aware of a freedom to choose. Brand Blanshard disagrees with Ross. "The feeling of freedom . . . is the feeling of an open future as regards the choice itself. . . . A sort of intuition stubbornly remains that we can not only lift our hand if we choose, but that the choice itself is open to us."[18] Blanshard maintains that we feel free even though our acts are caused, because our choices are made toward the future and not toward the past. Because of this factor, the feeling of freedom persists even though we may know the causes of our choice and that we could not have chosen otherwise.

Is a feeling of certitude adequate grounds for proving that a person could have chosen otherwise? Intuition as a method of inquiry has certain difficulties that make it unreliable as a way of knowing. We know from past experience that an individual can have a feeling of certitude about a certain belief, and yet the belief can be false. We also know that two people can have contradictory feelings of certitude about the same belief. Therefore, intuition is not a reliable source to prove that a person could have chosen otherwise.

Spinoza contended that choice is an illusion. There is nothing that exists objectively in the world that corresponds to what we feel when we say a man could have chosen otherwise. D. J. O'Connor asserts that choice is not an illusion.

> We cannot meaningfully talk of an illusory case of X unless there is a genuine case of X, just as we could not speak of "husbands" unless there were also "wives." . . . There must be at least one case of genuine free choice in the experience of anyone who is ever deceived in this way.[19]

O'Connor's argument is based upon the use of one of the meanings of *illusion*. In this sense, an illusion refers to a misleading appearance or image. That a particular appearance may be misleading implies there are cases where an appearance is genuine. For example, we cannot assert that the body of water we see before us is an illusion unless we have already experienced water. An illusion in sense one, that is, as a misleading appearance of X, does imply that a genuine case of X does exist. In sense two, an illusion is merely a false idea or conception that has no basis in reality. In sense two, an illusion does not imply that there is an actual case of X. If there were an actual case of X, then it would not be an illusion in sense two. Is choice an illusion in sense one or sense two? Choice is not an illusion in sense one. An illusion in this sense refers to a physical appearance. But choice is not a perception and therefore does not qualify as an illusion in sense one. Since choice is not analogous to illusion in sense one, it follows that O'Connor's argument is unsound.

Is it possible to empirically verify that a person could have chosen otherwise? It has been contended that if all circumstances were exactly the same today as when I made a certain choice ten years ago, I would act differently. Past experience has shown me that my original choice was unreasonable. But do we have the same conditions in these two situations? The fact that I mentioned that past experience has taught me something I did not previously know, means that the conditions in both situations were not exactly the same. My knowledge in the second situation was greater than my knowledge in the first situation.

When we ask whether a person could have chosen otherwise under these circumstances, we mean the same internal and external conditions under which the choice was made.

> Suppose I did act differently this time; suppose I didn't do the same thing on this hypothetical identical second occasion. Then you would automatically say that something had been different in the circumstances and that if nothing had been different I wouldn't or couldn't have acted differently! Your resolution not to admit exceptions is what makes your rule exceptionless.[20]

Hospers claims this is a mock battle. If we are going to make this an empirical battle, we cannot reject any evidence that will prove that a person could have chosen otherwise.

Some determinists have maintained that it is not necessary to resort to empirical data in order to determine whether an individual could or could not have chosen otherwise. Richard Taylor says that if determinism is true, then an individual could not have chosen otherwise. Why does it follow from the truth of determinism that an individual could not have chosen otherwise? Taylor asserts that if we accept determinism as true, "then we cannot avoid concluding that, given the causal conditions of those inner states, I could not have decided, willed, chosen, or desired otherwise than I in fact did, for this is a logical consequence of the very definition of determinism."[21]

The validity of Taylor's argument depends upon how he defines determinism. "Determinism is the thesis that whatever occurs occurs under conditions given which nothing else could occur. Indeterminism is simply . . . that at least some things occur under conditions given which something else could occur instead."[22] Taylor seems to be saying that determinism is the thesis that given certain initial conditions, one and only one event will follow. Indeterminism is the thesis that from a set of initial conditions, more than one event can follow.

If we accepted the concept of plurality of effects, then the thesis of determinism can be formulated in such a way that from a set of initial conditions, more than one event can follow. The soft and hard determinists are not using this concept of determinism in accepting or rejecting freedom and moral responsibility. They both define determinism to mean that from a set of initial conditions C, the event E invariably occurs. This definition of determinism is reducible to Taylor's formulation of determinism.

Why does it follow from this definition of determinism that an individual could not have chosen otherwise in the categorical sense? To maintain that an individual could have chosen otherwise means that, given these conditions, some other event would have occurred instead of the one that did occur. In other words, from a set of antecedent conditions, more than one event can occur. Determinism is the thesis that, from a set of antecedent conditions, one and only one event can follow. The categorical interpretation of *could have chosen otherwise* is a denial of determinism. Therefore, determinism is incompatible with the belief that an individual could have chosen otherwise in the categorical sense. If determinism is true, then it is false that an individual could have chosen otherwise. If an individual could have chosen otherwise, then he would be free in the sense that his initial choice was not caused. The hard determinist would deny that an individual is free in the sense that he could have chosen otherwise. The soft determinist rejects this definition of freedom, but he agrees with the hard determinist in denying that an individual could have chosen otherwise in the categorical sense.

What implications does the categorical interpretation of *could have chosen otherwise* have for moral responsibility?

The soft determinist would not accept this definition of moral responsibility, since determinism is incompatible with the categorical interpretation of *could have chosen otherwise*. To assert that a person could not have chosen otherwise is just another way of asserting that determinism is true. This fact does not negate the soft determinist's concept of moral responsibility. The hard determinist would deny that an individual is morally responsible in this sense, since it is incompatible with determinism.

The soft determinist claims that the hypothetical rendition of *could have acted otherwise* is compatible with determinism. The soft determinist concludes that man is morally responsible for those uncompelled acts in which it is true that he could have acted otherwise. The hard determinist would claim that although the hypothetical interpretation of *could have acted otherwise* is compatible with determinism, it does not justify his concept of moral responsibility. The fact that an act is uncompelled and that a person could have acted otherwise under different conditions does not satisfy the hard determinist's criteria of a responsible act.

CONCLUSION

IS MAN REALLY FREE? This question cannot be answered without certain preliminary definitions and criteria of free and responsible acts.

The soft determinist claims that if we define a free act as one that is voluntary and uncompelled, man is free and morally responsible. If an individual can fulfill his desires, and if he is not compelled by internal and external factors, he is free and morally accountable. The hard determinist denies that we are morally responsible, since our desires and our characters are caused by certain hereditary and environmental factors that we did not create. The soft determinist does not deny that an individual's character is ultimately caused by factors outside his control. There is no empirical dispute between the soft and hard determinists. The soft and hard determinists draw different conclusions from the observed facts. The soft determinist infers from these facts that man is free and morally responsible when his acts are voluntary and uncompelled. The fact that man's choices are ultimately the result of factors outside his control is irrelevant to the problem of determining when man is free and morally responsible. The hard determinist infers from these facts that man is not morally responsible, since his acts are ultimately caused by factors that he did not create. The hard determinist claims that the fact that an act is voluntary and uncompelled does not constitute a sufficient condition of moral responsibility.

The soft and hard determinists are using different senses of *free* and *moral responsibility* in their respective arguments. This is a form of equivocation that is sometimes called quibbling. Quibbling is a dispute where one individual argues for a particular conclusion, using a term in one sense, and another individual argues against this particular conclusion, using the term in a different way. The soft determinist maintains that, since man is free, he is morally responsible for his actions. Some hard determinists maintain that, since man is not free, he is not morally responsible. It appears as if the soft and hard determinists are disagreeing as to whether man is free, when actually they are using *free* in two different ways.

Who is quibbling about *free?* In one sense the hard determinist is quibbling on this term, and in another sense the soft determinist is quibbling. The hard determinist is quibbling when he states that we are not free because we did not choose our character and because our acts are ultimately caused by factors over which we have no control. For the soft determinist, we are free if our acts are uncompelled, and we are not free if our acts are compelled. The hard determinist is quibbling because he has argued against the conclusions of the soft determinist by using *free* and *moral responsibility* in a different sense. On the other hand, the soft determinist is quibbling when he argues against the hard determinist that we are in fact free at times. The soft determinist is quibbling because he is using a different sense of *free* in order to refute the position of the hard determinist.

The soft determinist is using a common use of *free* and *moral responsibility,* whereas the hard determinist is using a special sense of *free* and *moral responsibility* based on how some philosophers have used these terms historically. The soft and hard determinists are quibbling about a common use and a special use of *free* and *moral responsibility.* The quibble can be eliminated if the hard determinist decides to use the soft determinist's sense of *free* and *moral responsibility,* or if the soft determinist decides to use the hard determinist's concept of *free* and *moral responsibility.* Such an event is highly unlikely, since they both employ persuasive definitions of these terms. In this sense, the dispute between the soft and hard determinists is not purely verbal, since their definitions have important emotive consequences.

Words like *free* and *moral responsibility* have not only a descriptive meaning, but also an emotive meaning. If some-one wants to use or define a term in a special sense, he can stipulate a new descriptive meaning. When a new descriptive meaning is assigned to a term, the old emotive meaning is sometimes still preserved, despite the change of the descriptive meaning. In this case, if the old emotive meaning is used to persuade us to accept or reject a particular position, then a persuasive definition of a term has been employed. Although we can give a term a new descriptive meaning, we cannot stipulate a new emotive meaning. We can all be aware of a new or different designation of a term and still be misled by the emotive implications of the term.

When we examine the positions of the soft and hard determinists, we find that they have sometimes used persuasive definitions. The hard determinist contends that no one is morally responsible and that we should not blame anyone. No one is morally responsible because all our acts are ultimately caused by factors outside our control. The hard determinist uses the old emotive meaning of *not morally responsible* to support his definition. What the hard determinist has described is true, that is, all acts are ultimately caused by factors outside our control. By labeling this truth as *not morally responsible,* the hard determinist connects the feelings of sympathy, pity, understanding, and blamelessness with all acts. This is the emotive meaning of *not morally responsible* in the old sense.

Some hard determinists have maintained that we are not morally responsible because we could not have acted or chosen otherwise. Descriptively the phrase *could not have acted otherwise* means determinism is true, and yet emotively it implies that all acts are compelled, not blameworthy, and not punishable. The emotive meaning of *he could not have acted otherwise* or *he could not have helped it* is used to evoke sympathy for all acts and to lend support to the belief that we are not morally responsible.

The soft determinist states that man is free when his acts are uncompelled and he is not free when his acts are compelled. This concept of *free* flatters man's ego, and it makes him feel that he is sometimes the master of his own destiny. The soft determinist's definition of *not free* implies that the hard determinist is contending that all acts are compelled when he states they are not free. This definition is detrimental to the position of the hard determinist and favorable for the soft determinist. The soft determinist has equated the feeling of compulsion with the hard determinist's concept of *not free,* even though the hard determinist has not descriptively defined *not free* in this manner. It is interesting to note that some soft determinists have criticized hard determinism on the grounds that the position of hard determinism implies that all acts are compelled.

The soft determinist justifies blame in terms of effectiveness of punishment. *Blame* in this sense possesses the emotive implication of punishment, where *no blame* implies no punishment. This concept of blame is used advantageously to support the position of the soft determinist, since many people associate blame with punishment. On the other hand, it is detrimental to the position of the hard determinist. When a hard determinist maintains that no one is blameworthy, this emotively implies that no one should be punished under any circumstances. If no one is to be punished, this emotively implies that there should be no prisons and no laws. It also implies complete permissiveness and chaos. These emotive implications tend to support the soft determinist's concept of moral responsibility and to negate the hard determinist claim that no one is blameworthy.

These misleading emotive implications are responsible for some of the criticisms that have been made against the hard determinists. The hard determinist's contention that no one is blameworthy does not imply that no one should be punished. The deterrent and reformative theories of punishment are compatible with the hard determinist's contention that no one is blameworthy. *No blame* does not imply no prisons for the hard determinist. Prisons are places to confine certain people whose behavior is detrimental to society In this sense, we can evaluate the acts of people as being good or bad and can place them in prisons if necessary. This is compatible with the hard determinist's belief that no one is morally responsible or blameworthy.

These and other misleading emotive implications of certain terms account for some of the differences between the soft and hard determinists. The quibbling between the soft and hard determinists might be eliminated if they both used a neutral language to describe what they are saying.

Why has the free will problem never been solved? My analysis of the problem indicates that the free will problem will never be solved because of the distinct differences between the soft and hard determinists. The soft and hard determinists define *free* and *moral responsibility* in different ways. In this sense, the differences between the soft and hard determinists are not empirical, but rather linguistic. They are quibbling about the different senses of *free* and *moral responsibility*. The soft and hard determinists are also using persuasive definitions of *free* and *moral responsibility* in their respective arguments. The soft and hard determinists have different conceptions of what constitutes a sufficient condition of freedom and moral responsibility. In this sense, they differ about the criteria of a free and responsible act. The soft and hard determinists also employ different moral perspectives in determining whether an individual is morally responsible.

In one sense, we have solved the free will problem because we are now aware of the irreconcilable differences between the soft and hard determinists.

NOTES

❦

CHAPTER I

1. M. Schlick, "Causality in Everyday Life in Recent Science," in H. Feigl and W. Sellars, eds., *Readings in Philosophical Analysis* (New York: Appleton-Century-Crofts, 1949), 525.

2. M. Bunge, *Causality* (Cleveland: The World Publishing Company, 1959), 13.

3. A. Eddington, *The Nature of the Physical World* (New York: The Macmillan Company, 1929), 294.

4. S. Stebbing, *Philosophy and the Physicists* (London: Methuen & Co., Ltd., 1937), 183.

5. A. J. Ayer, *Foundations of Empirical Knowledge* (London: Macmillan and Co., Ltd., 1955), 214. Quotations from this work are reprinted by permission of St. Martin's Press, Inc., Macmillan and Co., Ltd., and The Macmillan Company of Canada, Ltd.

6. F. Hoyle, *The Nature of the Universe* (London: Basil Blackwell, 1952), 97ff.

7. J. Hospers, *An Introduction to Philosophical Analysis* (New York: Prentice-Hall, Inc., 1953), 261. © 1953 by Prentice-Hall, Inc. Quotations from this work are reprinted by permission of the publisher.

8. S. Hook, "Determinism," *Encyclopedia of the Social Sciences,* 5 (1931), 110-11.

9. C. A. Campbell, "In Defence of Free Will," in M. Munitz, ed., *A Modern Introduction to Ethics* (Glencoe: Free Press of Glencoe, Inc., 1958), 376.

10. C. A. Campbell, "Is 'Free Will' a Pseudo-Problem?" *Mind,* 60 (October, 1951), 459-60.

11. Campbell, "In Defence of Free Will," 379.

12. Campbell, "In Defence of Free Will," 380.

13. C. A. Campbell, *On Selfhood and Godhood* (London: George Allen & Unwin, Ltd., 1957), 169. Quotations from this work are reprinted by permission of the publisher.

14. Campbell, *On Selfhood and Godhood,* 177.

15. Campbell, *On Selfhood and Godhood,* 176.

16. Campbell, *On Selfhood and Godhood,* 177.

17. P. H. Nowell-Smith, "Determinists and Libertarians," *Mind,* 63 (July, 1954), 322.

18. Nowell-Smith, "Determinists and Libertarians," 322.

19. Nowell-Smith, "Determinists and Libertarians," 329-30.

20. P. H. Nowell-Smith, *Ethics* (London: Penguin Books, Ltd., 1954), 281. Quotations from this work are reprinted by permission of the publisher.

21. R. D. Bradley, "Free Will: Problem or Pseudo-Problem?" *Australasian Journal of Philosophy,* 36 (May, 1958), 41.

22. Bradley, "Free Will: Problem or Pseudo-Problem?" 42.

23. Bradley, "Free Will: Problem or Pseudo-Problem?" 42.

24. Campbell, *On Selfhood and Godhood,* 216.

25. Campbell, *On Selfhood and Godhood,* 216.
26. C. A. Campbell, "Free Will: A Reply to Mr. R. D. Bradley," *Australasian Journal of Philosophy,* 36 (May, 1958), 53.
27. Campbell, "Free Will: A Reply to Mr. Bradley," 53.
28. Campbell, "In Defence of Free Will," 381-82.
29. K. Lehrer, "Can We Know That We Have Free Will by Introspection?" *Journal of Philosophy,* 57 (March, 1960), 153.
30. Lehrer, "Can We Know That We Have Free Will by Introspection?" 155.
31. J. King-Farlow, "Mr. Bradley and the Libertarians," *Australasian Journal of Philosophy,* 37 (December, 1959), 237.
32. W. Hamilton, *Lectures on Metaphysics,* H. L. Mansel and J. Veitch, eds., Vol. II (London: Blackwood and Sons, 1870), 592.
33. F. Paulsen, *A System of Ethics,* trans. by F. Thilly (New York: Scribners and Sons, 1911), 459.
34. M. Schlick, *Problems of Ethics* (New York: Prentice-Hall, Inc., 1939), 154.
35. Nowell-Smith, *Ethics,* 282.
36. Nowell-Smith, *Ethics,* 283.
37. R. Taylor, "Determinism and the Theory of Agency," in S. Hook, ed., *Determinism and Freedom* (New York: New York University Press, 1958), 215-16. ©1958 by New York University. Quotations from this book are reprinted by permission of the publisher.
38. Taylor, "Determinism and the Theory of Agency," 216.
39. Campbell, *On Selfhood and Godhood,* 176.
40. C. Shute, "The Dilemma of Determinism After Seventy-Five Years," *Mind,* 70 (July, 1961), 337.

CHAPTER II

1. W. James, "The Dilemma of Determinism," in P. Edwards and A. Pap, eds., *A Modern Introduction to Philosophy* (Glencoe: Free Press of Glencoe, Inc., 1957), 329.
2. James, "The Dilemma of Determinism," 329.
3. R. E. Hobart, "Free Will as Involving Determinism and Inconceivable Without It," *Mind,* 43 (January, 1934), 16.
4. Hobart, "Free Will as Involving Determinism and Inconceivable Without It," 13.
5. J. Hospers, *An Introduction to Philosophical Analysis* (New York: Prentice-Hall, Inc., 1953), 271.
6. M. Schlick, *Problems of Ethics* (New York: Prentice-Hall, Inc., 1939), 147.
7. A. J. Ayer, "Freedom and Necessity," in A. J. Ayer, *Philosophical Essays* (London: Macmillan and Co., Ltd., 1954), 277.
8. Hospers, *An Introduction to Philosophical Analysis,* 271.
9. Schlick, *Problems of Ethics,* 150.
10. A. G. N. Flew, "Philosophy and Language," in A. G. N. Flew, ed., *Essays in Conceptual Analysis* (London: Macmillan and Co., Ltd., 1956), 19.
11. W. F. R. Hardie, "My Own Free Will," *Philosophy,* 32 (January, 1957), 21.
12. A. C. MacIntyre, "Determinism," *Mind,* 46 (January, 1957), 31.

13. Ayer, "Freedom and Necessity," 277.

14. B. Russell, *Portraits from Memory and Other Essays* (New York: Simon and Sch'uster, Inc., 1956), 167. © 1951, 1952, 1953, 1956 by Bertrand Russell. Reprinted by permission of the publisher.

15. R. C. Perry, "Professor Ayer's 'Freedom and Necessity,'" *Mind,* 70 (April, 1961), 233.

16. R. Handy, "Determinism, Responsibility, and the Social Setting," *Philosophy and Phenomenological Research,* 20 (June, 1960), 472.

17. Handy, "Determinism, Responsibility, and the Social Setting," 472-73.

18. H. Fain, "Prediction and Constraint," *Mind,* 67 (July, 1958), 369.

19. Fain, "Prediction and Constraint," 370.

20. M. Cranston, *Freedom: A New Analysis* (London: Longmans, Green & Co., Ltd., 1953), 131. Quotations from this work are reprinted by permission of Basic Books, Inc.

21. J. Laird, *On Human Freedom* (London: George Allen & Unwin, Ltd., 1947), 34. Reprinted by permission of the publisher.

22. J. Hospers, "Free Will and Psychoanalysis," in W. Sellars and J. Hospers, eds., *Readings in Ethical Theory* (New York: Appleton-Century-Crofts, 1952), 561.

23. Ayer, "Freedom and Necessity," 282.

24. Perry, "Professor Ayer's 'Freedom and Necessity,' " 231.

25. Edwards and Pap, eds., *A Modern Introduction to Philosophy,* 314-15.

26. MacIntyre, "Determinism," 33.

27. K. J. Scott, "Conditioning and Freedom," *Australasian Journal of Philosophy,* 37 (December, 1959), 219.

28. A. M. Munn, *Free Will and Determinism* (Toronto: University of Toronto Press, 1960), 202.

29. J. Wilson, "Freedom and Compulsion," *Mind,* 67 (January, 1958), 62.

30. P. Foot, "Free Will as Involving Determinism," *Philosophical Review,* 66 (October, 1957), 441.

31. Wilson, "Freedom and Compulsion," 64.

32. Ayer, "Freedom and Necessity," 280.

33. A. H. Maslow and B. Mittelman, *Principles of Abnormal Psychology* (New York: Harper and Brothers, 1951), 410.

34. "Kleptomaniacs and Thieves," *Science Digest,* (July, 1955), 33.

35. H. Weihofen, *The Urge to Punish* (New York: Farrar, Straus and Cudahy, 1956), 67. © 1956 by Henry Weihofen. Reprinted by permission of the publisher.

36. F. Alexander and H. Staub, *The Criminal, the Judge, and the Public* (New York: The Macmillan Company, 1931), 95-97.

37. D. R. Cressey, "The Differential Association Theory and Compulsive Crimes," *Journal of Criminal Law, Criminology and Police Science,* 45 (May-June, 1954), 35.

38. Schlick, *Problems of Ethics,* 152.

39. Schlick, *Problems of Ethics,* 153.

40. C. A. Campbell, "Is 'Free Will' a Pseudo-Problem?" *Mind,* 60 (October, 1951).

41. Campbell, "Is 'Free Will' a Pseudo-Problem?" 447.

42. S. Hook, "Moral Freedom in a Determined World," *Commentary,* 25 (May, 1958), 439.

43. Campbell, "Is 'Free Will' a Pseudo-Problem?" 447.

44. Hook, "Moral Freedom in a Determined World," 437.

45. P. H. Nowell-Smith, "Free Will and Moral Responsibility," *Mind*, 57 (January, 1948), 59.

46. Nowell-Smith, "Free Will and Moral Responsibility," 60.

47. M. Mandelbaum, "Determinism and Moral Responsibility," *Ethics*, 70 (April, 1960), 210. Reprinted by permission of the University of Chicago Press.

48. R. L. Franklin, "Dissolving the Problem of Free Will," *Australasian Journal of Philosophy*, 39 (August, 1961), 113.

49. D. D. Raphael, *Moral Judgment* (London: George Allen & Unwin, Ltd., 1955), 196. Reprinted by permission of the publisher.

50. R. L. Franklin, "Dissolving the Problem of Free Will," 114.

51. Cranston, *Freedom: A New Analysis*, 155.

52. Hook, "Moral Freedom in a Determined World," 439.

53. J. D. Mabbott, "Free Will and Punishment," in H. D. Lewis, ed., *Contemporary British Philosophy*, Third Series (London: George Allen & Unwin, Ltd., 1956), 297. Quotations from this work are reprinted by permission of the publisher.

54. H. Munsterberg, *On the Witness Stand* (New York: McClure Co., 1908), 259-60.

55. G. Aschaffenburg, *Crime and Its Repression* (Boston: Little, Brown and Company, 1913), 261.

56. K. F. Schuessler, "The Deterrent Influence of the Death Penalty," *Annals of the American Academy of Political and Social Science*, 284 (November, 1952), 54-62.

57. Aschaffenburg, *Crime and Its Repression*, 266.

58. A. C. Ewing, *The Morality of Punishment* (London: Kegan Paul, Trench, Truber & Co., 1926), 52.

59. Ewing, *The Morality of Punishment*, 80.

60. W. James, *Principles of Psychology*, Vol. II (New York: Henry Holt & Co., 1918), 549.

61. James, *Principles of Psychology*, Vol. I, 624.

62. K. G. Armstrong, "The Retributivist Hits Back," *Mind*, 70 (October, 1961), 484.

CHAPTER III

1. P. Edwards, "Hard and Soft Determinism," in S. Hook, ed., *Determinism and Freedom* (New York: New York University Press, 1958), 108-9.

2. C. A. Campbell, "Is 'Free Will' a Pseudo-Problem?" *Mind*, 60 (October, 1951), 456.

3. Edwards, "Hard and Soft Determinism," 110.

4. Edwards, "Hard and Soft Determinism," 111.

5. Edwards, "Hard and Soft Determinism," 112-13.

6. A. C. Danto, Review of *Determinism and Freedom*, S. Hook, ed., *Journal of Philosophy*, 56 (April, 1959), 371.

7. S. Hook, "Necessity, Indeterminism, and Sentimentalism," in S. Hook, ed., *Determinism and Freedom*, 174-75.

8. Hook, "Necessity, Indeterminism, and Sentimentalism," 175.

9. J. Hospers, *Human Conduct* (New York: Harcourt, Brace & World, Inc.,

1961), 516. Quotations from this work are reprinted by permission of the publisher.

10. Danto, Review of *Determinism and Freedom*, 371.

11. Danto, Review of *Determinism and Freedom*, 371-72.

12. R. Brandt, "Determinism and the Justifiability of Moral Blame," in S. Hook, ed., *Determinism and Freedom*, 142.

13. H. W. Hintz, "Some Further Reflections on Moral Responsibility," in S. Hook, ed., *Determinism and Freedom*, 164.

14. Hook, "Necessity, Indeterminism, and Sentimentalism," 175.

15. B. Spinoza, *Ethics*, trans. by R. H. M. Elwes, Vol. II (New York: Dover Publications, Inc., 1951), 189. Reprinted by permission of the publisher.

16. Hook, "Necessity, Indeterminism, and Sentimentalism," 177.

17. E. Nagel, "Some Notes on Determinism," in S. Hook, ed., *Determinism and Freedom*, 187.

18. H. Van Rensselar Wilson, "On Causation," in S. Hook, ed., *Determinism and Freedom*, 231.

19. S. Hook, "Moral Freedom in a Determined World," *Commentary*, 25 (May, 1958), 437.

20. Van Rensselar Wilson, "On Causation," 231.

21. E. L. Beardsley, "Determinism and Moral Perspectives," *Philosophy and Phenomenological Research*, 21 (September, 1960), 1-20.

22. J. Hospers, "Free Will and Psychoanalysis," in W. Sellars and J. Hospers, eds., *Readings in Ethical Theory* (New York: Appleton-Century-Crofts, 1952), 563.

23. Hospers, "Free Will and Psychoanalysis," 565.

24. J. Hospers, "What Means This Freedom?" in S. Hook, ed., *Determinism and Freedom*, 118.

25. Hospers, "Free Will and Psychoanalysis," 571.

26. Hospers, *Human Conduct*, 496.

27. Hospers, "What Means This Freedom?" 124.

28. Hospers, "What Means This Freedom?" 124.

29. Hospers, "What Means This Freedom?" 125.

30. Hospers, "What Means This Freedom?" 130.

31. S. Hook, "Necessity, Indeterminism, and Sentimentalism," 179.

32. Hospers, *Human Conduct*, 517.

33. Hintz, "Some Further Reflections on Moral Responsibility," 165.

34. Hospers, *Human Conduct*, 484.

35. P. A. Bertocci and R. M. Millard, *Personality and the Good* (New York: David McKay Co., Inc., 1963), 188.

36. Bertocci and Millard, *Personality and the Good*, 192.

37. F. S. C. Northrop, "Causation, Determinism, and the 'Good,'" in S. Hook, ed., *Determinism and Freedom*, 198.

38. H. Fingarette, "Psychoanalytic Perspectives on Moral Guilt and Responsibility: A Re-evaluation," *Philosophy and Phenomenological Research*, 16 (September, 1955), 30.

39. Fingarette, "Psychoanalytic Perspectives on Moral Guilt and Responsibility: A Re-evaluation," 31.

40. E. H. Madden, "Psychoanalysis and Moral Judgeability," in E. H. Madden, ed., *The Structure of Scientific Thought* (Boston, Houghton Mifflin Company, 1960), 348.

CHAPTER IV

1. G. E. Moore, *Ethics* (London: Oxford University Press, 1947), 127.
2. Moore, *Ethics*, 131.
3. P. H. Nowell-Smith, *Ethics* (London: Penguin Books, Ltd., 1954), 276.
4. Nowell-Smith, *Ethics*, 291.
5. J. L. Austin, "Ifs and Cans," in J. O. Urmson and G. J. Warnock, eds., *Philosophical Papers* (Oxford: Clarendon Press, 1961), 159.
6. Austin, "Ifs and Cans," 175.
7. Austin, "Ifs and Cans," 175.
8. Austin, "Ifs and Cans," 163.
9. P. H. Nowell-Smith, "Ifs and Cans," *Theoria*, 26 (Part 2, 1960), 87.
10. C. A. Campbell, *On Selfhood and Godhood* (London: George Allen & Unwin, Ltd., 1957), 163.
11. R. Taylor, "Determinism and the Theory of Agency," in S. Hook, ed., *Determinism and Freedom* (New York: New York University Press, 1958), 213.
12. P. H. Nowell-Smith, "Free Will and Moral Responsibility," *Mind*, 57 (January, 1948), 49.
13. J. D. Mabbott, "Free Will and Punishment," in H. D. Lewis, ed., *Contemporary British Philosophy*, Third Series (London: George Allen & Unwin, Ltd., 1956), 301.
14. H. D. Lewis, "Guilt and Freedom," in W. Sellars and J. Hospers, eds., *Readings in Ethical Theory* (New York: Appleton-Century-Crofts, 1952), 615-16.
15. C. A. Campbell, "Is 'Free Will' a Pseudo-Problem?" *Mind*, 60 (October, 1951), 453.
16. A. Pap, *Elements of Analytic Philosophy* (New York: The Macmillan Company, 1949), 59.
17. W. D. Ross, *Foundations of Ethics* (Oxford: Clarendon Press, 1939), 223-24.
18. B. Blanshard, "The Case for Determinism," in S. Hook, ed., *Determinism and Freedom*, 5.
19. D. J. O'Connor, "Is There a Problem About Free Will?" *Proceedings of the Aristotelian Society*, 43 (1948), 41.
20. J. Hospers, *An Introduction to Philosophical Analysis* (New York: Prentice-Hall, Inc., 1953), 275.
21. R. Taylor, *Metaphysics* (Englewood Cliffs: Prentice-Hall, Inc., 1963), 44.
22. Taylor, "Determinism and the Theory of Agency," 211.

BIBLIOGRAPHY

༃

Books

Adler, M. J. *The Idea of Freedom*. 2 vols. Garden City, Doubleday & Company, Inc., 1961.

Berlin, I. *Historical Inevitability*. London, Oxford University Press, 1954.

Berofsky, B., ed. *Free Will and Determinism*. New York, Harper & Row, Publishers, 1966.

Bertocci, P. A., & Millard, R. M. *Personality and the Good*. New York, David McKay Co., Inc., 1963.

Bunge, M. *Causality*. Cleveland: The World Publishing Company, 1959.

Campbell, C. A. *On Selfhood and Godhood*. London, George Allen & Unwin, Ltd., 1957.

Cranston, M. *Freedom: A New Analysis*. London, Longmans, Green and Co., Ltd., 1953.

Davidson, M. *The Free Will Controversy*. London, C. A. Watts & Co., Ltd., 1942.

Enteman, W. F., ed. *The Problem of Free Will*. New York, Charles Scribner's Sons, 1967.

Ewing, A. C. *The Morality of Punishment*. London, Kegan Paul, Trench, Truber & Co., 1926.

Farrer, A. *The Freedom of the Will*. New York, Charles Scribner's Sons, 1958.

Hook, S., ed. *Determinism and Freedom*. New York, New York University Press, 1958.

Hospers, J. *An Introduction to Philosophical Analysis*. New York, Prentice-Hall, Inc., 1953.

———. *Human Conduct*. New York, Harcourt, Brace & World, Inc., 1961.

Laird, J. *On Human Freedom*. London, George Allen & Unwin, Ltd., 1947.

Lehrer, K., ed. *Freedom and Determinism*. New York, Random House, Inc., 1966.

Moore, G. E. *Ethics*. London, Oxford University Press, 1947.

Morgenbesser, S., and Walsh, J., eds. *Free Will*. Englewood Cliffs, Prentice-Hall, Inc., 1962.

Munn, A. M. *Free Will and Determinism*. Toronto, University of Toronto Press, 1960.

Nowell-Smith, P. H. *Ethics*. London: Penguin Books, Ltd., 1954.

Pap, A. *Elements of Analytic Philosophy*. New York, The Macmillan Company, 1949.

Pearl, L. *Four Philosophical Problems*. New York, Harper & Row, Publishers, 1963.

Pears, D. F., ed. *Freedom and the Will*. New York, St. Martin's Press, Inc., 1965.

Raphael, D. D. *Moral Judgment*. London, George Allen & Unwin, Ltd., 1955.

Ross, W. D. *Foundations of Ethics*. Oxford, Clarendon Press, 1939.

Schlick, M. *Problems of Ethics*. New York, Prentice-Hall, Inc., 1939.

Stevenson, C. L. *Ethics and Language*. New Haven, Yale University Press, 1944.

Taylor, R. *Metaphysics*. Englewood Cliffs, Prentice-Hall, Inc., 1963.

Articles and Essays

Armstrong, K. C. "The Retributivist Hits Back," *Mind*, 70 (October, 1961), 471-90.

Aune, B. "Abilities, Modalities, and Free Will," *Philosophy and Phenomenological Research*, 23 (March, 1963), 397-413.

Austin, J. "Ifs and Cans," in Urmson, J. O., & Warnock, G. J., eds., *Philosophical Papers*. Oxford, Clarendon Press, 1961, 153-80.

Ayer, A. J. "Freedom and Necessity," in Ayer, A. J. *Philosophical Essays*. London, Macmillan and Co., Ltd., 1954, 271-84.

Beardsley, E. L. " 'Excusing Conditions' and Moral Responsibility," in Hook, S., ed., *Determinism and Freedom*. New York, New York University Press, 1958, 133-37.

———. "Determinism and Moral Perspectives," *Philosophy and Phenomenological Research*, 21 (September, 1960), 1-20.

Blanshard, B. "The Case for Determinism," in Hook, S., ed., *Determinism and Freedom*. New York, New York University Press, 1958, 3-15.

Bradley, R. D. "Free Will: Problem or Pseudo-Problem?" *Australasian Journal of Philosophy*, 36 (May, 1958), 33-45.

Brandt, R. "Determinism and the Justifiability of Moral Blame," in Hook, S., ed., *Determinism and Freedom*. New York, New York University Press, 1958, 137-43.

Broad, C. D. "Determinism, Indeterminism, and Libertarianism," in Broad, C. D., *Ethics and the History of Philosophy*. London, Routledge and Kegan Paul, Ltd., 1952, 195-217.

Campbell, C. A. "Is 'Free Will' a Pseudo-Problem?" *Mind,* 60 (October, 1951), 441-65.

———. "Free Will: A Reply to Mr. R. D. Bradley," *Australasian Journal of Philosophy,* 36 (May, 1958), 46-56.

———. "In Defense of Free Will," in Munitz, M., ed., *A Modern Introduction to Ethics.* Glencoe, Free Press of Glencoe, Inc., 1958, 375-86.

Cressey, D. R. "The Differential Association Theory and Compulsive Crimes," *Journal of Criminal Law, Criminology and Police Science,* 45 (May-June, 1954), 29-40.

Danto, A. C. "The Paradigm Case Argument and the Free-Will Problem," *Ethics,* 49 (January, 1959), 120-24.

———. Review of *Determinism and Freedom,* Hook, S., ed., *Journal of Philosophy,* 56 (April, 1959), 369-73.

Dore, C. "On the Meaning of 'Could Have'" *Analysis,* 23 (December, 1962), 41-43.

Edwards, P. "Hard and Soft Determinism," in Hook, S., ed., *Determinism and Freedom.* New York, New York University Press, 1958, 104-13.

Fain, H. "Prediction and Constraint," *Mind,* 67 (July, 1958), 366-78.

Fingarette, H. "Psychoanalytic Perspectives on Moral Guilt and Responsibility: A Re-evaluation," *Philosophy and Phenomenological Research,* 16 (September, 1955), 18-36.

Foot, P. "Free Will as Involving Determinism," *Philosophical Review,* 66 (October, 1957), 439-50.

Franklin, R. L. "Dissolving the Problem of Free Will," *Australasian Journal of Philosophy,* 39 (August, 1961), 111-24.

Gallagher, K. T. "On Choosing to Choose," *Mind,* 73 (October, 1964), 480-95.

Garnett, A. C. "Freedom and Responsibility in Moore's Ethics," in Schilpp, P. A., ed., *The Philosophy of G. E. Moore.* Chicago, Northwestern University Press, 1942, 177-99.

Gustafson, D. F. "Voluntary and Involuntary," *Philosophy and Phenomenological Research,* 24 (June, 1964), 493-501.

Handy, R. "Determinism, Responsibility, and the Social Setting," *Philosophy and Phenomenological Research,* 20 (June, 1960), 469-76.

Hardie, W. F. R. "My Own Free Will," *Philosophy,* 32 (January, 1957), 21-38.

Hedenius, I. "Broad's Treatment of Determinism and Free Will," in Schilpp, P. A., ed., *The Philosophy of C. D. Broad*. New York, Tudor Publishing Company, 1959, 579-96.

Hintz, H. W. "Some Further Reflections on Moral Responsibility," in Hook, S., ed., *Determinism and Freedom*. New York, New York University Press, 1958, 163-67.

Hobart, R. E. "Free-Will as Involving Determinism and Inconceivable Without It," *Mind*, 43 (January, 1934), 1-27.

Honoré, A. M. "Can and Can't," *Mind*, 73 (October, 1964), 463-79.

Hook, S. "Determinism," *Encyclopedia of the Social Sciences*, 5 (1931), 110-14.

———. "Moral Freedom in a Determined World," *Commentary*, 25 (May, 1958), 431-43.

———. "Necessity, Indeterminism, and Sentimentalism," in Hook, S., ed., *Determinism and Freedom*. New York, New York University Press, 1958, 167-80.

Hospers, J. "Meaning and Free Will," *Philosophy and Phenomenological Research*, 10 (March, 1950), 307-30.

———. "Free Will and Psychoanalysis," in Sellars, W., & Hospers, J., eds., *Readings in Ethical Theory*. New York, Appleton-Century-Crofts, 1952, 560-75.

———. "What Means This Freedom?" in Hook, S., ed., *Determinism and Freedom*. New York, New York University Press, 1958, 113-30.

James, W. "The Dilemma of Determinism," in Edwards, P., & Pap, A., eds., *A Modern Introduction to Philosophy*. Glencoe, Free Press of Glencoe, Inc., 1957, 327-40.

Kaufman, A. S. "Moral Responsibility and the Use of 'Could Have,'" *Philosophical Quarterly*, 12 (April, 1962), 120-28.

Kenner, L. "Causality, Determinism and Freedom of the Will," *Philosophy*, 39 (July, 1964), 233-48.

King-Farlow, J. "Mr. Bradley and the Libertarians," *Australasian Journal of Philosophy*, 37 (December, 1959), 234-38.

Ladd, J. "Free Will and Voluntary Action," *Philosophy and Phenomenological Research*, 12 (March, 1952), 392-405.

Lehrer, K. "Can We Know That We Have Free Will by Introspection?" *Journal of Philosophy*, 57 (March, 1960), 145-57.

Lewis, H. D. "Guilt and Freedom," in Sellars, W., & Hospers, J., eds., *Readings in Ethical Theory*. New York, Appleton-Century-Crofts, 1952, 597-620.

Locke, D. "Ifs and Cans Revisited," *Philosophy,* 37 (July, 1962), 245-56.

Mabbott, J. D. "Punishment," *Mind,* 48 (April, 1939), 152-67.

———. "Free Will and Punishment," in Lewis, H. D., ed., *Contemporary British Philosophy,* Third Series. London, George Allen & Unwin, Ltd., 1956, 289-309.

———. "Free Will," *Encyclopedia Britannica,* 9 (1963), 746-50.

MacIntyre, A. C. "Determinism," *Mind,* 46 (January, 1957), 28-41.

Madden, E. H. "Psychoanalysis and Moral Judgeability," in Madden, E. H., ed., *The Structure of Scientific Thought.* Boston, Houghton Mifflin Company, 1960, 340-49.

Mandelbaum, M. "Determinism and Moral Responsibility," *Ethics,* 70 (April, 1960), 204-19.

Matson, W. I. "On the Irrelevance of Free-Will to Moral Responsibility, and the Vacuity of the Latter," *Mind,* 65 (October, 1956), 489-97.

Moore, G. E. "A Reply to My Critics," in Schilpp, P. A., ed., *The Philosophy of G. E. Moore.* Chicago, Northwestern University Press, 1942, 535-677.

Nagel, E. "Some Notes on Determinism," in Hook, S., ed., *Determinism and Freedom.* New York, New York University Press, 1958, 183-88.

Northrop, F. S. C. "Causation, Determinism, and the 'Good,'" in Hook, S., ed., *Determinism and Freedom.* New York, New York University Press, 1958, 188-99.

Nowell-Smith, P. H. "Free Will and Moral Responsibility," *Mind,* 57 (January, 1948), 45-61.

———. "Determinists and Libertarians," *Mind,* 63 (July, 1954), 317-37.

———. "Ifs and Cans," *Theoria,* 26 (Part 2, 1960), 85-101.

O'Connor, D. J. "Is There a Problem About Free Will?" *Proceedings of the Aristotelian Society,* 43 (1948), 33-46.

———. "Possibility and Choice," *Proceedings of the Aristotelian Society,* Suppl., 34 (1960), 1-24.

Perry, R. C. "Professor Ayer's 'Freedom and Necessity,'" *Mind,* 70 (April, 1961), 228-34.

Pitcher, G. "Necessitarianism," *The Philosophical Quarterly,* 11 (July, 1961), 201-12.

Russell, L. J. "Ought Implies Can," *Proceedings of the Aristotelian Society,* 36 (1935-36), 151-86.

Schlick, M. "Causality in Everyday Life and in Recent Science," in Fiegl, H., & Sellars, W., eds., *Readings in Philosophical Analysis*. New York, Appleton-Century-Crofts, 1949, 515-33.

Scott, K. J. "Conditioning and Freedom," *Australasian Journal of Philosophy*, 37 (December, 1959), 215-20.

Shute, C. "The Dilemma of Determinism After Seventy-Five Years," *Mind*, 70 (July, 1961), 331-50.

Skinner, R. C. "Freedom of Choice," *Mind*, 72 (October, 1963), 463-80.

Smart, J. J. C. "Free Will, Praise, and Blame," *Mind*, 70 (July, 1961), 291-306.

Taylor, R. "Determinism and the Theory of Agency," in Hook, S., ed., *Determinism and Freedom*. New York, New York University Press, 1958, 211-18.

————. "I Can," *Philosophical Review*, 69 (January, 1960), 78-89.

University of California Associates. "The Freedom of the Will," in Feigl, H., & Sellars, W., eds., *Readings in Philosophical Analysis*. New York, Appleton-Century-Crofts, 1949, 594-615.

Van Rensselar Wilson, H. "On Causation," in Hook, S., ed., *Determinism and Freedom*. New York, New York University Press, 1958, 225-31.

Wienpahl, P. D. "Concerning Moral Responsibility," *Analysis*, 13 (June, 1953), 127-35.

Williams, G. "Free Will and Determinism," *Journal of Philosophy*, 38 (December, 1941), 701-12.

Wilson, J. "Freedom and Compulsion," *Mind*, 67 (January, 1958), 60-69.

Zimmerman, M. "Is Free Will Incompatible With Determinism?" *Philosophy and Phenomenological Research*, 26 (March, 1966), 415-20.

INDEX

❦

Alexander, F., 35, 94n36
Armstrong, K. G., 47, 95n62
Aschaffenburg, G., 44, 95n55
Austin, J. L., 76–79, 97n5–8
Ayer, A. J., 4, 22, 24–25, 30–31, 34–35, 92n5, 93n7, 94n13, 23, 32

Beardsley, E. L., 61, 96n21
Bertocci, P. A., 69–71, 96n36
Blame: vagueness of meaning, 40, 60; justification of, 36; in relation, to the dead, 39; to animals, 37–38; to children, 38, 55; persuasive definition of, 89–90
Blanshard, B., 82, 97n18
Bradley, R. D., 10–11, 92n21, 22
Brandt, R., 56, 96n12
Bunge, M., 2, 92n2

Campbell, C. A., 7–16, 37–38, 50, 52, 79–81, 92n9–16, 93n24–28, 39, 94n40, 41, 95n43, 97n10, 15
Causality: principle of, 4–5; uncaused events, 5; libertarian concept of, 7; Hospers on, 21; soft determinist concept of, 9
Character: choosing our *original*, 50, 53; cognitive meaning of our *original*, 53–54; concept of luck, 65–67; heredity and environment, 65–67. *See also* Libertarianism
Choice, 28–29, 61, 83
Classical physics: and quantum physics, 3; Eddington on, 3–4
Compulsion: and causation, 19, 21, 23; and freedom, 23–25, 27, 29–36; and predictability, 27–28; and voluntary acts, 28–29; posthypnotic behavior, 29; kleptomania, 29–35 *passim;* and events, 30–31; and conditioning, 32; external and internal, 33–34; and unconscious causes, 62–63
Constraint. *See* Compulsion
"Could have": hypothetical

interpretation, 75–78; relation of meaning to "would have, if," 76–78; relation of meaning to "should have, if," 75, 77; categorical interpretation, 79–86; verification of categorical sense of, 83–84; and moral responsibility, 85–86; implications for soft and hard determinism, 85–86
Cranston, M., 27–28, 42, 94n20, 95n51
Cressey, D. R., 34–35, 94n37
Criminal behavior: and punishment, 43–47; and moral responsibility, 56–57; and the social order, 56–57; the treatment approach, 59

Danto, A. C., 51, 52, 55, 96n10, 11
Darrow, C., 51
"Dilemma of Determinism, The" (James), 17
Determinism: definition of, 2; and predictability, 2; indeterminism, 3–5; justification of, 4–6; as a leading principle, 6; presupposition of inquiry, 6; and moral responsibility, 6, 36–40, 50–51; and fatalism, 18–19, 68–69; compatibility with freedom, 18–23; and descriptive and prescriptive laws, 21–22

Eddington, A., 3–4, 92n3
Edwards, P., 31–32, 48–58, 64, 95n1, 3–5
Ewing, A. C., 44, 95n58

Fain, H., 27, 94n18, 19
Fatalism. *See* Determinism
Fingarette, H., 72–74, 96n38, 39
Flew, A. G. N., 93n10
Foot, P., 33, 94n30
Franklin, R. L., 41–42, 95n48, 50
Free and free will. *See* Freedom
Freedom: reportive definition of, 22–23; and compulsion, 23–36

ABOUT THE AUTHOR

EDWARD D'ANGELO, a native of New York, has received degrees from the State University College at Oswego (B.S., 1954), New York University (M.A., philosophy, 1958; M.A., philosophy of education, 1959), and the State University of New York at Buffalo (Ph.D., philosophy, 1966), and he served as assistant professor of philosophy at the State University College at Buffalo. While a member of the faculty of the University of Missouri—Kansas City, he received an Assistant Professor Research Grant to evaluate the literature on the teaching of critical thinking (February 1—August 31, 1968). His research in this area is continuing, on the postdoctoral level, at Cornell University in Ithaca, New York.

In addition to this study, Professor D'Angelo has published "The Myth of Soviet Education" (*Humanist Bulletin,* February, 1961) and "Observations of Soviet Education" (*Balanced Living,* April, 1961).